winning
Ugly | 44
DO NOT DRY CLEAN-WASH IN COLD WATER
WITH MILD SOAP. DO NOT USE BLEACH.

winning

Ugly

A VISUAL HISTORY OF BASEBALL'S MOST UNIQUE UNIFORMS

TODD RADOM

SPORTS PUBLISHING

Sports Publishing books may be purchased in bulk at special discounts for sales promotion, corporate gifts, fund-raising, or educational purposes. Special editions can also be created to specifications. For details, contact the Special Sales Department, Sports Publishing, 307 West 36th Street, 11th Floor, New York, NY 10018 or sportspubbooks@skyhorsepublishing.com.

Sports Publishing® is a registered trademark of Skyhorse Publishing, Inc.®, a Delaware corporation.

Visit our website at www.sportspubbooks.com.

10 9 8 7 6 5 4 3 2

Library of Congress Cataloging-in-Publication Data is available on file.

Cover design and illustrations by Todd Radom

All photographs, unless otherwise noted, are courtesy of AP Images.

All illustrations are courtesy of the author. All uniform photographs are courtesy of the Bill Henderson collection.

Print ISBN: 978-1-68358-395-0
Ebook ISBN: 978-1-68358-229-8

Printed in China

For Susanne
whose advice was "write, then keep writing."

Table of Contents

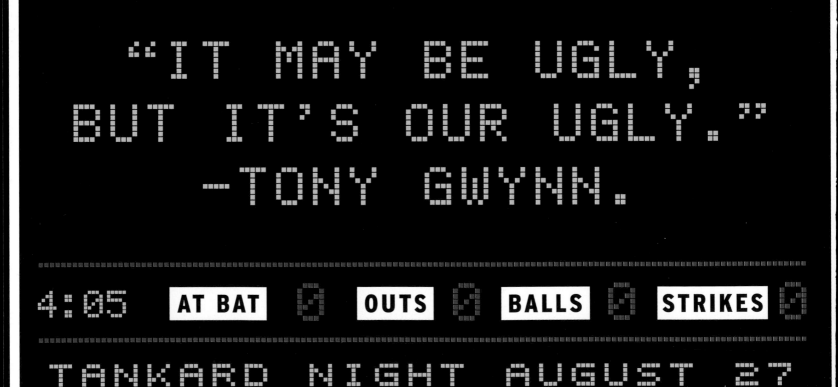

"IT MAY BE UGLY, BUT IT'S OUR UGLY."
-TONY GWYNN.

4:05 | AT BAT | 0 | OUTS | 0 | BALLS | 0 | STRIKES | 0

TANKARD NIGHT AUGUST 27

Introduction

Cooperstown, New York, rightly calls itself "America's perfect village," a point that few could argue. Its picturesque two-block-long Main Street parallels the southern end of Lake Otsego, a serene 7.8-mile-long body of water that writer James Fenimore Cooper accurately dubbed "Glimmerglass."

While its apocryphal status as the birthplace of baseball has long been debunked, Cooperstown, of course, plays host to the National Baseball Hall of Fame and Museum, which first opened its doors in the summer of 1939.

Every year, hundreds of thousands of visitors enter the Federal-style red brick building at 25 Main Street and immerse themselves in the history of the game—but only a fortunate few can access its secure, climate-controlled storage area, located deep in the bowels of the facility.

Anyone lucky enough to gain entry to this area comes away with the distinct sense that this would be the ideal place to survive a nuclear attack.

I will omit certain details. There are some mysteries that should remain a secret, but trust me, this is an exceptionally special place.

Walk past the gallery of iconic bronze plaques. Enter a door, head down a flight of steps. There, a long hallway beckons, followed by more heavily protected doors. You sign in. Finally, you enter a room. You then don a pair of white protective gloves.

You are then overcome by an eerily calm sensation, enveloped in a cool chill, accompanied by absolute silence.

The room is, at first glance, impossibly white. The floors and walls are light in color. Tall stacks of archival white boxes loom. Within them reside game-worn examples of some of the most spectacular uniforms in the history of the sport.

Here's a creamy flannel jersey, embellished with wide navy blue pinstripes, worn by some New York Giant player over a century ago. Over there is a thick gray wool number, replete with laces, upon which sits the bold decoration of a red sock with the word "Boston" within it, an impossibly rare game-worn example from 1908. And here, resting quietly, is another uniform from 1908, worn by a member of the World Series champion Chicago Cubs, featuring a black felt letter "C," looped around a dyspeptic-looking bear cub holding a baseball bat.

These jerseys are stunningly beautiful.

This book is not about those jerseys.

Professional baseball teams have been tinkering with their on-field look for a century and a half. Along the way, there have been hits, and there have been misses.

Baseball, more than any other sport, lends itself to introspection and observation. The season is a marathon. It begins in Spring Training in February or March, and it concludes with the final out of the World Series in the final days of October, if not the first week of November.

For many baseball fans, their relationship to their favorite team begins with the uniform. As comedian Jerry Seinfeld famously observed, the players come and go, teams sometimes move from city to city, and fans end up "rooting for the clothes."

This is a book for those of us who look at those clothes with interest. Sometimes this interest is akin to watching a dumpster erupt in flames, transfixed by what's happening, all the while a little nervous at what the end result might be.

It's a tribute to the sheer chutzpah of whomever it was that decided that the Pittsburgh Pirates should wear a dizzying combination of black and gold uniforms that made them look for all the world like a swarm of bumblebees.

This is for everyone who, like me, knows that once upon a time, the Padres looked like tacos and that the Astros wore tequila sunrises, that the White Sox swathed themselves in leisure suits, and that once upon a time in Cleveland, Boog Powell resembled a giant blood clot.

In today's globalized society, one can purchase and consume the same Big Mac in nearly 120 different countries. Much of America looks alike, and quirky regional differences have largely disappeared. Remember the 1977 film *Smokey and the Bandit*? The core plot revolves around a scheme to bootleg four hundred cases of contraband Coors beer, then unavailable east of the Mississippi River, from Texas to Georgia. Today this seems ridiculous; Coors is ubiquitous, easily obtained just about anywhere.

For all of our political and social differences, we are, at long last, a pretty monolithic society when it comes to our consumer culture, and sports is a key part of that. There are still provincial holdouts to be sure, but there once was a time when the Montreal Expos sure as hell looked like they came from a French-speaking country and when the San Diego Padres gave off a strong whiff of Taco Bell, a Southern California fast-food culinary staple.

These were the halcyon days of pet rocks and "Gee Your Hair Smells Terrific," of streakers and of string art. This was a time when our sports graphics and uniforms were more joyful and more spontaneous, before they were mass-produced by behemoth apparel companies whose primary focus is and will always be the almighty, focus-tested bottom line.

I am a child of the seventies, born in the waning days of The Baby Boom. My parents took me to the 1964 New York World's Fair in a stroller. Some of my earliest school memories involve watching Apollo moon shots in elementary school on a big black and white television, an event so spectacularly noteworthy that it warranted a temporary halt to the school day.

I was born in New York City and I vividly remember the summer of 1977. That was the Summer of Sam, the summer of the blackout, and the summer that I watched the expansion Toronto Blue Jays and Seattle Mariners, resplendently attired in their powder blue road uniforms, get crushed by the mighty Bombers at Yankee Stadium in the Burning Bronx.

The ticket stubs tell the story. My great-uncle Gus, a resident of Inwood in Upper Manhattan, was an avid New York Giants fan until his team deserted him for the City by the Bay and broke his heart. He then became an avid Mets fan, much to the chagrin of his Yankee-loving wife, Mildred. On July 16, 1977, a mere four days after the great blackout, he took me to Shea Stadium to see the Mets play the Pirates on Old Timer's Day. I sat in loge section 30, box 474A, Seat 3. The stub depicts a despondent Mr. Met, a single tear trickling down from the right eye of his big round head, hoisting an umbrella: the rain check area of the ticket.

There was no need for tears that day. Willie, Mickey, the Duke, *and* Joe D were all there, and the putridly awful Mets, already buried, 18 games out of first place, defeated Pittsburgh 5–3. I remember Willie Stargell absolutely crushing a home run to left-center and I vividly recall the Bucs' uniforms. They wore gold jerseys and pants that hot afternoon, topped off by their bizarre, black, striped, cakebox flat-top caps, a stylistic holdover from the bicentennial season prior.

More ticket stubs. May 7, 1978, Yankees vs. Texas; powder blue road uniforms with henley buttons. Game One of the 1977 American League Championship Series, Bombers vs. Royals, who wore powder blue pullovers that read "KANSAS CITY" in white letters that were really hard to see from a distance. Mets/Phillies, a solid team with crystal blue Drano roadies. Yanks vs. A's; Kelly green and gold, a jarring contrast to the soberly attired home club. The list goes on and on, and my memories of the visitors are written in strikingly brilliant hues, a memorably chromatic smorgasbord of doubleknit goodness.

Four decades later, I am a fourth generation working artist. My late father was a big Yankees fan, a creative jack-of-all-trades who did a lot of commercial photography in the seventies, including a shoot for a sporting goods catalog at the original Yankee Stadium, sometime in the fall or early winter of 1972, a year before the place was torn apart for renovations. My parents pulled me out of school that day to tag along and I distinctly remember having the run of the cavernous empty ballpark. We walked around the fabled Monuments, then squarely in the field of play in left-center, looking remarkably like grave markers for pinstriped heroes of the distant past.

The models that day were all major league players, lesser guys on the Mets and Yankees, and the uniforms that they modeled were all polyester pullovers with generic team names. I still have the auto-graphed Polaroids—Dave Marshall, Tug McGraw, Jim McAndrew. They are all sporting really, really hideous jerseys. Duffy Dyer, the Mets' catcher, is wearing a pinstriped number with wide red bands around the neck and sleeves that reads "Buccaneers." His signature is light years more stylish than his uniform.

Ron Blomberg would become the first designated hitter in MLB history a year later with the Yan-kees, but the photo from this particular day depicts him in a burnt orange jersey that says "Athletics," rendered in chunky script letterforms, black with a white outline. And Danny Frisella, a righty reliever, is shod in a harshly pinstriped jersey with enormously bulky trim that reads "Washington College." Frisella died in a dune buggy accident in Arizona on New Year's Day, 1977.

I have a tattered paper portfolio that somehow survived high school, college, multiple moves, and the all that the ensuing years brought forth to bear. In it are a series of drawings, mostly done in color ballpoint Bic pens and magic markers. They are, in retrospect, pretty good for a teenager. They de-pict, in trompe l'oeil style, hanging uniforms, team pennants, and various team-lettered tchotchkes, all carefully and accurately depicted in the appropriate colors of the era. The word PIRATES is carefully drawn in yellow against black, and the San Francisco Giants' script uniform lettering of the time bears a more than reasonable resemblance to the real deal, black with a white outline against an orange background.

I attended college at the School of Visual Arts in New York. During my first two years there I lived on the tenth floor of the Sloane House YMCA, a mammoth structure that still stands on the southeast corner of 34th Street and 9th Avenue. The school had two floors, surrounded on all sides by a city that had been in a period of deep decline for some time. These were the beginning years of the crack epidemic, in a dirty city with a failing transit system and more than two thousand murders per annum.

Amidst all of this I resided a couple of hundred steps away from Madison Square Garden, then, as now, one of the principal epicenters of New York City sports. In those days there was a store over toward the 7th Avenue end of the Garden called Gerry Cosby's, a venerable sporting goods retailer that supplied uniforms to the New York Knicks and Rangers. Cosby's was a uniform geek's paradise, a cluttered emporium containing hundreds of examples of official jerseys and jackets, as well as all sorts of cool sporting equipment.

My visits through the store, usually made every couple of days, brought me face-to-face with a sea of polyester team outfitting, a real rarity in the days before the Dick's Sporting Goods of the world sold this kind of stuff everywhere. It mattered not that my art school budget prevented me from actually buying anything; I was there to ogle the merchandise, and I partook in this exercise with great delight.

It was at this time that I was lucky enough to fall in with a group of fellow students who were sports fans, just like me, and since it was art school, we discussed the optics of the games we watched with fervent enthusiasm. After graduation we began to take baseball road trips. Remember, dear reader, that this was the dark ages, several years before there was a thing called the Internet. A road trip like this took some planning, and that planning had nothing to do with securing lodging, which represented little more than a spontaneous afterthought.

The key logistics involved looking at how the MLB schedule stacked up, usually in a printed newspaper at the beginning of the season, and seeing how many different games we could hit in a particular weekend. We once rented a car in Jersey and drove to Kansas City for a three-day weekend, with a detour to see the Cardinals play in St. Louis along the way. It's probably important to point out the fact that the distance between Hoboken, New Jersey, and Kansas City, Missouri, is approximately 1,190 miles, or nearly 2,400 miles round trip. In three days. With two baseball games in between.

In 1988 we crossed the border to see the Expos and their funny tricolor hats, and we also drank a lot of Molson Brador beer. We drove to Toronto to see the Blue Jays and their wonderfully modern uniforms at weird Exhibition Stadium, hard by the shores of Lake Ontario. It was there that we sat on cold metal bleacher benches and I was shat upon by a seagull. Seeing the crisp white Jays' home uniforms in person more than made up for that small inconvenience.

Half a lifetime later we are close friends still, and our remembrances of these times are, of course, accompanied by our recollections of the uniforms that we saw.

There soon came a point that my appreciation for and my understanding of what teams wore became my professional calling. My design work has now appeared on the uniforms of every major-league club over the past quarter century, including those funny-lidded Expos, stolen away to Washington, DC, in 2005 and reborn as the Nationals. As a matter of fact, I was the guy who designed the Nationals' first visual identity, including their uniforms.

Go ahead and hate me, but I was also the one who redid the logo and uniforms of the Milwaukee Brewers back in 1994, replacing the now beloved "ball-in-glove" look. Back then it was considered dated and ugly, derided as looking like a dog's paw print and associated with years of crappy baseball. Memories are currency, and nostalgia tends to soften the hard edges of what might have at one time been considered grotesque.

While I love and appreciate the classics—the Cardinals, Red Sox, Yankees, and Tigers immediately spring to mind—there is a warm place in my heart for some of the truly questionable uniforms that I grew up with. For many years now I have been assisting both Major League Baseball and the National Baseball Hall of Fame and Museum in Cooperstown, helping to research and make digital the logos and uniform decorations that have graced (and sometimes disgraced) the diamond over the long history of professional baseball.

Along the way I have learned of some delightful disasters of distant years past. I've also come to appreciate the fact that people care deeply about this stuff and have since the very genesis of the sport.

The history of professional baseball stretches back to 1869, the year that the American continent was united by the first transcontinental railroad. The Civil War had ended four years earlier, and the American flag then featured thirty-seven stars. Pundits have been opining on baseball uniforms ever since then, assessing the optics of the game in sometimes scathing fashion.

A 1908 item from *Sporting Life* noted, "(w)ithin the last few years there has been a tendency toward the garish in base ball uniforms. There's too much of this insignia and curlicue business. The only really artistic diamond apparel brought out in recent seasons was that of the Pittsburg club."

Everything sucks. Change is bad. Strip away some of the florid language and you essentially have an online comment that would not be unfamiliar today.

Here in the third decade of the twenty-first century, fans have an unprecedented number of uniform options to love and to hate, to gripe about and to embrace with partisan fervor. And yet, as is the case with anything aesthetic, there is no right or wrong answer.

What makes for a great baseball jersey? Conversely, what is it about a certain uniform that causes it to be damned as something that's ugly? This is all very subjective stuff, of course.

I think it's instructive to look to Supreme Court Justice Potter Stewart, who, in a 1964 case involving the definition of obscenity, famously opined, "I know it when I see it."

Justice Stewart was a passionate fan of the Cincinnati Reds. He passed away in October 1985, long before his beloved team sported camouflage jerseys, a look that he most likely would have found to have been in contempt of court.

Tastes shift, trends come and go (and often come back again).

There are, however, some looks that have endured as perennial favorites, classics through thick and thin. The New York Yankees' home uniform is probably the most obvious example.

The Yankees' home suit has been the subject of praise and adulation since the team first donned pinstripes and an interlocking "NY" in 1912. They dropped the stripes for a couple of years and then restored them for good in 1915. The "NY" went missing for nearly two decades. Hard as it is to believe, Babe Ruth never wore the famed "NY" on the front of his uniform as a player, ever.

The Bronx Bombers' home look is all business, like a bespoke pinstriped wool suit that never goes out of style. It's timeless and effortless, steeped in tradition, dripping with gravitas, along with a heaping side of mystique. It's old money; as a matter of fact, it practically *reeks* of money, a fitting wardrobe for the financial juggernaut that was long ago compared to that soulless, cash-generating monopoly, US Steel.

Some uniforms benefit from a "halo effect." Winning helps. A tradition of winning can help elevate a uniform through lean years on the field of play.

The Yankee pinstripes connect Babe Ruth to Lou Gehrig to Joe DiMaggio—straight down the line to Mantle, Reggie, Mariano, and Jeter. Winning lifts perceptions.

When the Yankees bottomed out for a couple of years in the early 1990s, fans could still look forward to seeing Joe D, Yogi, Mickey, and Whitey in the famed pinstripes on Old Timer's Day, an enduring, tangible connection to better times.

Similarly, the Dodgers' crisp home whites link Jackie Robinson and Sandy Koufax to Clayton Kershaw and the Dodgers of the early twenty-first century.

LA's classic look bridges the entire American continent, having originated during their time in Brooklyn, in 1938. That season Larry MacPhail, newly installed as the Dodgers' executive vice president and general manager, decided to ditch the Kelly green togs that the club wore the previous year.

The new uniforms featured the word "Dodgers," rendered in an upward-facing, underscored script, delivered in a clean royal blue that has come to serve as the visual cornerstone of the franchise.

Red player numbers were later added to the fronts of the uniforms, a touch that represented the finishing brushstrokes on a baseball masterpiece. There's a story here that needs to be told. The Dodgers first appeared with red numbers on their uniform fronts in 1952, but they were originally scheduled to have made their debut during the 1951 World Series.

The only problem was that the Dodgers never made it to the 1951 World Series, having been painfully crushed by Bobby Thomson's "Shot Heard 'Round the World," arguably the most famous home run in the history of baseball. This historic homer propelled their hated rivals, the New York Giants, to the Fall Classic that year. The Giants had overcome a 12 1/2 game deficit to catch Brooklyn and eventually beat them in a three-game playoff series.

In April 1952, the *Sporting News* ran an article that discussed the red digits, saying that they were the brainchild of Dodgers owner Walter O'Malley. It noted that the innovation would be "of particular benefit to television fans who often obtain only a front view of a player before he passes out of the camera range. The stunt is one of good will to the public and while we would like to be able to report that this is an innovation from 1952, actually the story is the result of an unhappy ending. These uniforms were made for the Dodgers to wear in the 51 series!"

The red numbers were added for added visibility on black and white TVs, a huge consideration for the club as they began to market themselves to the new national mass media of television.

Out of pain came gain, and the result was what many observers feel is THE quintessential baseball uniform. Ross Yoshida is one such observer, and somewhat of an expert witness, even if he's biased.

Yoshida is the Dodgers' Director of Graphic Design. He is also a Los Angeles native who has rooted for his team since he was a kid. He says that one of the things that make the club's home whites an all-time classic is the script wordmark.

"The bold script 'Dodgers' with the tail flourish screams 'baseball' to me," he says. "The element that makes the Dodger uniform 'classic' to ME is the contrasting red number on the front of the jersey. It brightens the jersey, offers a visual break in the white/blue, and has been a signature piece of the Dodger uniform since 1952. If you see a blue script with a red number on the front of a baseball jersey, you immediately think 'Dodgers.'"

He is, of course, correct.

On the other hand, there are plenty of examples of uniforms that have been ridiculed, mocked, and despised, right out of the chute.

When the 1963 Kansas City Athletics bucked tradition and took the field clad in green and gold, news accounts called them "outlandish," "utterly silly," "gaudy," and reminiscent of "a women's softball team."

Yogi Berra, as always, brought some sage perspective and logic to the discussion when, on Opening Day, he noted of the A's, "they must like them because they're wearing them."

Some ugly uniforms gain equity with the passing of time. Nostalgia is a powerful narcotic, and now, more than ever, fans are looking for comfort food when it comes to our sports identities.

As of right now the current century has been a dark one, marred by years of economic anxiety, political and societal upheaval, and a pervasive atmosphere of uncertainty. These days, when it comes to our sports brands, we want a big bowl of mashed potatoes and gravy. Give us a heaping helping of meatloaf, thank you. Seconds, even. Baltimore Orioles fans want their smiling bird. Milwaukee Brewers fans cannot get enough of their vintage ball-in-glove logo. The Chicago White Sox and Pittsburgh Pirates, for example, wear throwback uniforms on a regular basis, alternate uniforms that are trotted with regularity, a tacit assurance that, even in a topsy-turvy world, everything is going to be just fine.

Several years ago the Toronto Blue Jays rightfully restored order when they dropped their dark, monochromatic uniforms for an updated version of their original look. This move was embraced with fervent enthusiasm. Give the people what they want and everybody goes home happy.

Today, many view the San Diego Padres' brown and gold look of the 1970s and 1980s with great fondness. A powerful grassroots movement to "bring back the brown" paid off in 2020, when the club restored that color as their primary hue—a forceful example of just how much fans care about the optics of their favorite teams.

In 1990, Tony Gwynn, who is now commemorated with a statue that rightly calls him "Mr. Padre," said, "I love wearing the brown and orange, as ugly as it is." Twenty-two years later, Gwynn told ESPN, "brown is part of who the Padres are." It may have been ugly, but it's *OUR* ugly.

Nostalgia seems to roll in twenty-year cycles. The 1970s brought us *Happy Days* and *American Graffiti*. *That '70s Show* first aired in 1998, and Generation X's cultural consciousness revolves around all things nineties.

All of this, of course, begs the question: What does the future of the baseball uniform look like? We live in a world chock full of diminished attention spans and 24/7 news cycles, of abbreviated communication that's often expressed via emojis and emoticons. The answer could well look like college football's Oregon Ducks.

The University of Oregon's football team is known as a laboratory of experiment for Nike, that little apparel company that's located just up the road in Beaverton. In 2006, Oregon's suite of uniforms provided 384 potential different combinations of helmets, jerseys, pants, socks, and footwear. Just a few years later the number of combinations exceeded five hundred.

As of 2020, Nike is the new official on-field outfitter of Major League Baseball, a potentially seismic event that could very well redefine what the silhouette of a baseball uniform looks like. Given the economic dynamics of the relationship, it seems like an opportune moment for a massive rethinking of the uniform. Will we return to sansabelt pants? How about the elimination of buttons, a vestigial feature that seems decidedly useless, if time-honored.

Whatever the future holds, we can be sure that fans will absorb the optics of the outfits and chime in with likes, dislikes, snark, and praise. Let's hope it's at least interesting, and let's hope that somewhere in the mix we get an opportunity to build upon the memorably great sartorial dumpster fires of years past.

—Todd Radom
January 2020

In the Beginning . . .

The first organized baseball club, the New York Knickerbockers (no, not *those* New York Knicker-bockers), adopted a standard uniform in 1849, one that consisted of blue woolen pants, white flannel shirts, and straw hats. (They would switch to mohair caps a few years later.)

But baseball's first *professional* team, the Cincinnati Red Stockings, gets credit for having invented the baseball uniform that we are familiar with today.

On July 15, 1867, the Cincinnati club took the field against the Washington Nationals clad in what the *Cincinnati Enquirer* called "dress white caps, white shirts, white pants, and red belt and leggin(g)s." This uniform would essentially serve as a template for every baseball uniform worn since.

Cincinnati's look became famous as the club toured the nation and sliced through their competition like a hot knife through butter. The following year the *Brooklyn Daily Eagle* described the Red Stockings' uniforms as "of white flannel trimmed with red, a red belt and stockings, the pants being fastened at the knee." It also noted the fact that "their uniform received many complimentary comments."

The club's use of knee-length knickerbocker pants represents an innovation that reverberates to this day. This decision turned out to be an inspired one, for it opened the door to yet another sartorial trademark, the use of flashy knee-high stockings, so worthy of note that it gave birth to the teams' nickname.

The club's signature hosiery turned out to be a stroke of marketing genius. It was also quite controversial at the time.

Team president Aaron Champion later remembered:

"Now, be it known that knickerbockers, to-day so common—the showing of the manly leg in varied-colored-hose—were unheard of, and when [team captain] Harry Wright occasionally appeared with the scarlet stockings, young ladies' faces blushed as red, and many high-toned members of the club denounced the innovation as immoral and indecent."

* * *

Two men can reasonably lay claim to being the father of baseball uniform design.

One is George B. Ellard, a founding member of the Red Stockings. Ellard, who was born in Ireland in 1820, was a thirty-third-degree mason and an avid sportsman. He served as president of Cincinnati's Union Cricket Club and helped secure their home grounds for the freshly minted base ball club in 1867.

In 1907, Ellard's son, Harry, wrote a definitive tome on the history of baseball in Cincinnati, appropriately titled *Base Ball in Cincinnati*. He drew upon his father's collection of "books, scores, photographs, and documents," and specifically cites his dad as having created the club's distinctive look.

Is this an example of a son trying to puff up his father's legacy? It's possible, but there are older accounts of George Ellard having been the sole member of the Red Stockings to actually *wear* red stockings—in 1866, prior to them becoming a formally recognized component of the club's attire.

There's more. George Ellard owned a sporting goods store, located very close to today's Cincinnati Reds home ballpark. In 1870, Ellard published a team schedule, backed by an ad for his "Base Ball Emporium," located at 28 West Fourth Street in Cincinnati. It boasted of having "the largest stock in the west of base ball goods."

This 1875 advertisement clearly seeks to leverage the Red Stocking connection:

The other serious contender is Harry Wright.

The English-born Wright was an important pioneer in the annals of early baseball. A cricketer like Ellard, Wright was the first openly paid baseball player ever. He managed the all-professional 1869 Red Stockings to a perfect 57–0 record, and went on to found the Boston Red Stockings in 1871—the distant ancestors of today's Atlanta Braves.

Wright's bronze plaque at the National Baseball Hall of Fame and Museum in Cooperstown, New York, specifically

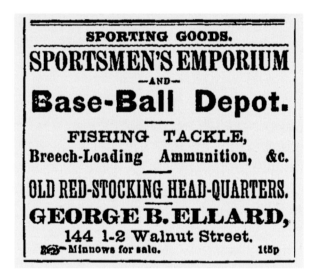

SPORTING GOODS.

SPORTSMEN'S EMPORIUM

—AND—

Base-Ball Depot.

FISHING TACKLE,
Breech-Loading Ammunition, &c.

OLD RED-STOCKING HEAD-QUARTERS.

GEORGE B. ELLARD,
144 1-2 Walnut Street.

Minnows for sale.   1t5p

If the Ellard claim is taken as fact, then he is the George Washington of baseball uniform design. His Betsy Ross, according to *Base Ball in Cincinnati*, is Bertha Bertram, a Cincinnati seamstress. Harry Ellard wrote "the orders for the manufacture of the uniforms for the nines of 1867-68-69-70 were given by Mr. Ellard to Mrs. Bertha Bertram."

says that he "introduced knicker uniforms." Wright himself took credit for the whole thing, specifically in an 1875 interview with the *Cincinnati Enquirer* in which he states: "I would like to say . . . that the uniform I used as (a) cricketer was adopted by the base-ball club."

Wright's brother, George, is also a Hall of Famer, and is sometimes described as "baseball's first super-star." George credited his brother with the innovation in an interview he gave to the *Boston Herald* in 1888:

> My brother Harry first brought about this important change, and it was somewhat in this manner: The Young America Cricket Club of Philadelphia used often to come to New York, where my brother then was, to play games, and on one of its trips, in the year 1865, the captain of the cricket club presented my brother with a pair of long red stockings. In the succeeding year, 1866, when my brother went on his western trip, he took these stockings with him, and also had made for him a pair of knickerbocker pants to go with them.

Whatever the case, the Red Stockings style caught on. Some teams continued to employ "shield-front" jerseys, which resembled those worn by firefighters of the era. Others wore jerseys with laces. Eventually, buttons became the accepted style, a feature that has ruled the baseball world ever since (with the notable exception of the 1970s, which we will get to later).

While most discourse on the togs of this era were full of praise, some uniform sets gave rise to snarky derision.

One such early example is that of the 1872 Baltimore club of the National Association, the first pro league. The team was described by the *Chicago Inter Ocean* as "clad in yellow pants, white shirts, white hats, and ugly looking black and yellow stockings."

The stockings featured a distinctive diamond pattern, similar to that of Maryland's state flag. The yellow pants, however, inspired all sorts of colorful nicknames for the team, including "Mustard Trowsers," "Yellow Legs," and "Dandelions."

In 1882, the National League adopted a league-wide rule, which called for players at each position on the field to wear a different color uniform. Every team featured a catcher clad in scarlet, a right fielder in gray, a first baseman in scarlet and white stripes, and so on. Team identification was limited to stocking colors, with Buffalo in gray, Cleveland in navy blue, et al.

1872 MUSTARD TROUSERS

Uniform critics of the day jumped all over the look. The *Detroit Free Press* said, "this will give a rainbow hue to the diamond and make the spectators wish they were color blind." Later in the season the same paper referred to them as "clown costumes."

The *Buffalo Commercial* checked in with the following: "(t)he League will abolish the 'Harlequin uniforms' at the next annual meeting. Rumor says next year the players will appear in tights like circus performers. Then some of the more athletic members may be expected to turn double somersaults on their way to first, second or third base." As predicted, the league surrendered, abandoning the experiment by the middle of June.

The 1888 American Association Cincinnati Reds took the field of play with a set of alternate uniforms that echoed the NL's failed exercise of six years earlier, with a completely different uniform for just about every player on the sixteen-man roster.

These togs—termed "parti colored"—were form fitting and tight, a departure from the baggy flannels that fans of the era were accustomed to seeing.

Catcher Jim Keenan's jersey had blue and black stripes, third baseman Hick Carpenter trotted out in red and black stripes, and shortstop Frank Fennelly wore solid maroon.

First baseman Long John Reilly, a lanky 6-foot-3 slugger, wore red and white stripes, of which the *Baltimore Sun* said, "(i)n his new uniform of red and white stripes Long John Reilly looks like an elongated stick of peppermint candy."

Louisville was the Reds' big rival of the era, and the *Louisville Journal-Courier* noted that the local nine "seemed to delight in making the Cincinnatis slide in the mud," thus spoiling their fancy outfits.

As the old saying goes, all good things must end, and the era of colorful, sometimes outlandish, often gaudy major-league uniforms piffed out as the 1880s concluded.

While the following decade produced several conspicuous outliers, it was, for the most part, a sedate affair, with little in the way of experimentation or noteworthy color. The outerwear of the 1892 Boston

Beaneaters, defending and eventual National League champs, did inspire some memorable snark when *Sporting Life* referenced their "detestable convict striped sweaters of red and black."

*   *   *

The nineteenth century gave way to the twentieth. The American League established itself as a legitimate outfit, thus joining the well-established National League in what we now know as "the majors." Visually speaking, this was a flat, somnolent time, characterized by boring graphics and little variety in the way of color.

The 1905 Chicago Cubs set the standard for boring with their home uniforms, which were devoid of anything—no trim, no lettering, no nothing. Floppy collars ruled the day, and pockets on jerseys were still a thing. It should be noted that numbers first came to major league uniforms in 1916, followed by player names in 1960, so these Cubs togs were truly drab.

Amidst this vast sea of sameness were a few green shoots of interesting outliers. Praise must be given to legendary New York Giants manager John McGraw, a Hall of Famer and an enthusiastic uniform tinkerer. McGraw's Giants took the field for the first game of the 1905 World Series clad all in black, a look that he again trotted out for the club's 1911 Fall Classic appearance. His club pioneered collarless jerseys in 1906—ones that boldly spelt out the words "WORLD'S CHAMPIONS." In 1913, McGraw commissioned violet-trimmed uniforms, a vivid tribute to New York University's signature color.

The 1916 Giants were outfitted in uniforms that the *Philadelphia Inquirer* termed "peculiar." The *St Louis Post-Dispatch* opined that the Giants "may or may not be the best ball club in the world, but we'll say this for them: They have the ugliest uniforms in either league." Beauty, as the saying goes, is in the eye of the beholder. Giants' traveling secretary John B. Foster pronounced them "the last word in baseball sartorial invention."

That year the Giants, along with their National League neighbors, the Brooklyn Robins, took the field in uniforms that featured a checkered pattern, an odd-looking experiment that was soon shelved.

To contemporary eyes, baseball's distant past often seems shrouded in sepia-toned mythology, a Ken Burns production loaded with bushy mustaches and thick, flannel uniforms. A closer examination, however, reveals some real surprises, including some stylistic experiments that are best left dead and buried.

This is the uniform that begat all baseball uniforms—behold the crimson-legged Cincinnati Red Stockings—the first professional baseball club, world-beaters, and fashion pioneers. The Red Stockings originated the use of knickerbocker pants and decorative hosiery, thus setting the tone for every baseball uniform since. (Wikimedia Commons)

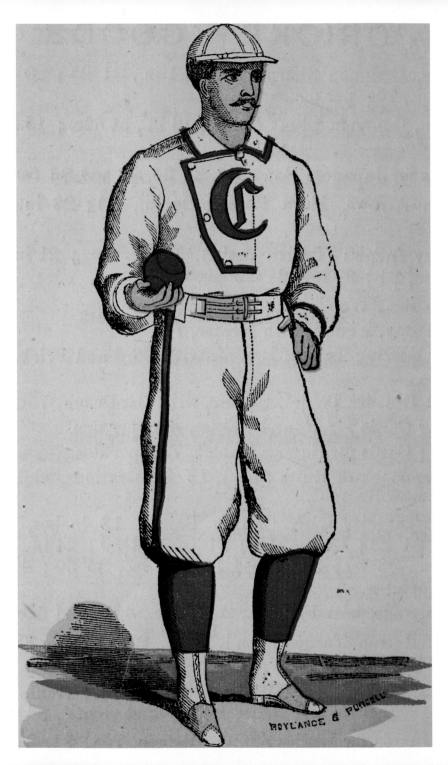

Behold the uniforms of the 1876 St. Louis Brown Stockings, charter members of the National League. There is so much about this photo to observe—the Greek keyed collars and belts, the ornate Victorian furniture, all that casual lounging about—all of which help contribute to the sneaking suspicion that these men are waiting to be transported a hundred years distant, only to be repurposed as blackjack dealers at Caesar's Palace in Las Vegas. (Public domain)

Jack "Moose" Farrell's eleven big-league seasons included stops in long forgotten National League cities such as Providence and Syracuse, but his finest moment is depicted here, in the uniform of the 1887 Washington Statesmen, a.k.a. Nationals, a.k.a. Senators.

Farrell, seen pointing at the camera, is doing many things here. He is tagging out a would-be base-stealer, and seems to have forgotten to bring his fielders mitt. He is standing astride an improvised second base, which, upon closer inspection, appears to be an unfolded table napkin. Finally, he is stylishly attired in his Washington uniform, the most visible component of which is a wide white belt, a future staple of men's fashion some nine decades after this photo was taken. (Library of Congress)

JOHN WEYHING, P. Athletics
COPYRIGHTED BY GOODWIN & CO. 1888
OLD JUDGE
CIGARETTES.
GOODWIN & CO., New York.

'OLD JUDGE Cigarettes

DORGAN, R. F. N. Y's.
COPYRIGHTED BY GOODWIN & CO. 1887.
GOODWIN & CO. New York.

This baseball card is literally a work of art, even if the uniform that it depicts is somewhat odd and unattractive. It is one of thirty thousand baseball cards that are part of the Metropolitan Museum of Art's Jefferson R. Burdick Collection, and it depicts pitcher Harry Coveleski. Harry enjoyed a solid MLB career, but his lone season in this all-blue Cincy road uniform was 1910, a year in which he appeared in seven games, including one in which he walked 16 batters. This feat earned him a one-way ticket to Chatanooga.

The Reds sported these blue uniforms on the road for several years prior to World War I, a look that, in retrospect, seems like a precursor to the stone-washed denim craze that hit big some seven decades later. (Library of Congress)

COVELESKI CINCINNATI

In 1916, both the New York Giants and Brooklyn Robins (later known as Dodgers), separated by 13 miles or so, decided to embark upon a weird look, busting out uniforms that featured a checkered pattern.

Brooklyn's checks were tightly spaced and rendered in blue, while New York's formed more of a crosshatched plaid and were executed in a violet or purple color.

The Giants went 26 consecutive games without a loss that September, but the Robins won the National League pennant and the theoretical Checkered Uniform Championship of the City of New York for 1916. (Library of Congress)

In 1906, the American League's St. Louis club—the Browns—donned ornately detailed uniforms, trimmed in black. The shift in team colors caused several local newspapers to dub the team the "Ravens."

After winning six American League pennants during the circuit's first 14 years, Connie Mack's Philadelphia Athletics fell on hard times. Seeking a change in fortune, the club dropped the familiar Old English "A" from their uniforms in 1920. In its place lumbered a crudely rendered visage of an elephant, depicted in an optimistically prosperous green color.

The Athletics had been associated with pachyderms since the earliest days of the franchise, but this one afforded them little in the way of either optics or fortune. The club went 48–106 in 1920, and scrapped both the uniforms and the color green after that one single season.

Here are several members of the 1925 Chicago White Sox, resplendent in their navy blue road uniforms with head-to-toe white pinstripes. A sharp look for a double-breasted suit, not so much for a baseball uniform.

Chicago won the 1918 NL pennant while wearing these road uniforms, which featured a blocky horizontally stretched logo that looks like it says "UBS." The uniforms were described as "melancholy drab" and were trimmed in green, which led some newspapers to refer to them as the "Green Sox."

In Living Color

When it comes to sports, color is everything. Sports fans are tribal in nature. Colors help to both define team identities and to propel sales of licensed merchandise. Colors help to delineate rivalries. Sports colors, akin to the colors of national flags, are a key piece of the visual culture of teams and their groups of fans.

The official rules of Major League Baseball state, "a league may provide that each team shall wear a distinctive uniform at all times, or that each team shall have two sets of uniforms, white for home games and a different color for road games."

This has traditionally been interpreted as "white at home, gray on the road." It's been a visible and reliable part of baseball since the late nineteenth century, but those rules haven't always applied.

Back in the days of handlebar mustaches and horseless carriages, a handful of teams went with dark togs while on the road, generally navy blue or black. In 1901, for instance, the American League's Baltimore Orioles wore black jerseys and pants on the road, accompanied by snazzy yellow and black striped socks.

Vibrant, or even dark-colored baseball uniforms, began to depart the diamonds of Major League Baseball during the first decade of the twentieth century.

In 1909, the *Rochester Democrat and Chronicle* ran an article entitled "Uniforms of Rainbow Hues Given Release." It noted "(c)olor is passing from the baseball field. . . . White and gray are soon to be the color schemes of the big-league clubs.

"The love for color, which is more or less barbarian, has passed into baseball history."

The Chicago White Sox wore dark blue while traveling from 1902–15. It took a World War to make them switch to the more conventional gray, as explained (with pithy commentary) in the March 25, 1916, edition of *Sporting Life:*

"The White Sox will not wear dark blue road uniforms this year. One reason for the change is that that the scarcity of dyes, owing to the war in Europe, makes it difficult to get good blue cloth. A silver lining to the war cloud."

Tight supplies of blue dye must have loosened up the following year, because on Opening Day 1917, in St. Louis, the Sox took on the Browns in uniforms that were described as "blue with white pencil stripes." That look was forsaken after a few brief months.

As the twenties roared on, Major League Baseball got bogged down in a dull sea of white and gray, with only the White Sox to help break things up, again going with navy blue on the road for a few years in the latter part of the decade and the first couple years of the thirties.

America struggled through the Great Depression. The on-field look of baseball did nothing at all to help brighten things up. The Cincinnati Reds did their part, going with flaming-red pants for a couple night games in 1936, but the world of big-league baseball was a dreary-looking one as the thirties gave way to the forties.

And then—behold! A flash of color emerged from the Midwest. The Chicago Cubs, to the ridicule of many, stepped forward with powder blue road uniforms, unveiling them on June 30, 1941, in a game in Cincinnati against the Reds.

"Have the Cubs developed a pantywaist inferiority complex?" asked the *Sporting News.*

The look was both ridiculed *and* short-lived, as the Cubs reverted back to gray in 1943.

The following year, the Brooklyn Dodgers went all-in with satin powder blue uniforms for select night games while on the road. These were used sparingly, and then discarded for good, once again relegating the world of big-league ball to bleak, desolate monotone.

*   *   *

World War II concluded, the atomic age beckoned, the Cold War raged. The suburbs boomed, Elvis gyrated his way to fame and fortune, and humankind rocketed toward space, orbiting a blue planet that was populated by baseball uniforms of white and gray.

There are times in the course of history when man and moment collide, thus changing the course of human events. One individual, someone with vision, the clarity of knowing that he is right, and the confidence to speak truth to power, can serve as a singular catalyst for such a change.

That man was Charles Oscar Finley, and his rendezvous with destiny took place in 1963. Paraphrasing the words uttered by President John F. Kennedy just two years earlier, the glow from the fire he lit did truly light the world.

That year Finley unleashed a plan that shook the colorless world of baseball to its core, propelling it into the jet age and changing the look of the game for always and forever.

Finley sought permission from the American League to dress his team in vivid green and gold uniforms at home—and, in a total break from tradition, *white* on the road. He correctly observed something that few, if any, of his fellow team owners saw—that color was a very important thing when it came to selling entertainment.

"My feeling," he said, "is that baseball should do everything possible to add color to the game."

Finley said that he chose green and gold in honor of his favorite college football team, Notre Dame.

As it worked out, his Athletics would wind up wearing "Tulane gold" uniforms, trimmed with Kelly green, for *all* games, both at home and on the road: the first shot in a Technicolor revolution that resonates to this very day.

Finley was a man ahead of his time. He was a visionary and a marketing genius, a self-made millionaire with an eye for color and a gift for promotion that both stunned and angered his fellow team owners. He was combative, contentious, and, above all, colorful—the perfect individual to drag baseball out of its fusty aesthetic doldrums and into the modern era.

Nancy Finley literally grew up around the Athletics franchise. Her father, Carl, was both cousin and right-hand man to Charlie, serving in a wide variety of key positions, including Executive Vice President for nearly a quarter century.

"Charlie was all about color—literally," she notes.

"After our first 1971 playoff series, I heard Charlie say 'our colors need to be deeper.'" That offseason the uniforms were changed to a deeper, darker green, a look that coincided with the A's three consecutive World Series wins in 1972, '73, and '74.

Nancy takes inventory of her uncle's clear obsession for adding color to the game. "A royal blue second base? Orange baseballs? Peacocks roaming our stadium in Kansas City? Sheep dyed various colors, grazing above our bleacher seats, with a shepherd wearing a brightly striped robe?"

She has a theory. Nancy is certain that her uncle had synesthesia, a neurological condition in which different senses are mixed—letters and numbers, in this instance, would be strongly associated with vivid and specific colors.

By her reckoning, Charlie Finley literally had a sixth sense when it came to color.

"It seems obvious, now," she says, "that Charlie was a synesthete. When he heard certain numbers or words he pictured associated colors, a condition possessed by a tiny fraction of the population. One neurologist called it 'cerebral cross-talk.'"

The first year of baseball's chromatic revolution was not an easy one for Finley and his team. Ralph Houk, manager of the buttoned-up World Series champion Yankees, called the Athletics' outfits "screwball uniforms." Houk, serving as manager of the American League squad in that summer's All-Star Game, declined to play Norm Seibern, the A's lone All-Star selection, supposedly because he felt that the green and gold getups were an affront to the entire league.

Various news accounts called them "bizarre" and "clownish," and the players were tarred with descriptors such as "organ grinder's monkeys" and "girls softball players."

On the other hand, legendary sportswriter Red Smith called them "gorgeous," adding "it goes to show what intelligent ownership can do for a team."

As if to add fuel to an already smoldering fire, Finley added player names—mostly in the form of nicknames—to the backs of the jerseys in early June. Pitcher Dave Wickersham's jersey, logically enough, read "Wick." Along the same lines, future Boston Red Sox owner Haywood Sullivan got "Sully," and pitcher Bill Fischer was dubbed "Fish."[1]

Infielder Ed Charles would gain fame six years later as a member of the "Miracle Mets," and would go on to be called "the Glider," but in 1963, his jersey simply read "Ed."

Jerry Lumpe got "Lump." Howard Edwards was "Doc," and so on down the line.

While there was no getting around the fact that nicknames on uniforms were just one piece of Finley's promotionally driven schtick, there was also a practical reason for the departure. The Athletics' jerseys were vests, with a compressed area between the shoulder blades for names. Every name had to be five letters or less in order to fit, which meant that fans could see future Hall of Fame manager Tony La Russa play, secure in the knowledge that his first name was, in fact, "Tony."

Some players professed embarrassment, but others went along for the ride. In a nice complementary

---

1 While the Chicago White Sox pioneered the use of player names in 1960, the Athletics built upon their burgeoning reputation as uniform mavericks with this much-discussed addition.

touch, outfielders Ken "Hawk" Harrelson and Gino Cimoli rose to the occasion with green and gold bats.

The Athletics' uniforms garnered all sorts of attention that year, but their play was less than noteworthy. The team finished 16 games under .500 and in eighth place, but no matter. The seeds had been sown for a visual transformation that would elevate the look of baseball in the coming decades in ways that were scarcely imaginable to just about anyone other than Charlie O. Finley.

Some years later, Finley told the *New York Times* "(w)hen colored uniforms were considered the work of a heretic, I stood up. I knew the system of home whites and road grays couldn't continue."

He was right.

* * *

"Après moi le deluge."
—French quotation attributed to Louis XV
or Madame de Pompadour

In October 1963, the Yankees and Dodgers faced off in the World Series, clad in flannel uniforms that would have looked familiar to those who were alive the first time those teams faced off in the fall classic some two decades earlier.

A month later, President Kennedy was assassinated in Dallas. A nation mourned.

A new year beckoned, and with it, the promise of renewed hope. Four young British fellows with funny haircuts made music and took the world by storm.

As baseball looked forward to Spring Training, the fire that Finley lit jumped the tracks and moved northward, to Chicago. That January, the White Sox announced that they would be wearing powder blue flannels on the road, a look last worn by the Cubs thirty years prior.

Sox general manager Ed Short noted that powder blue would look better on black and white televisions, solidly pragmatic reasoning that might well have been designed to soften the inevitable blow of public opinion.

Finley, who never let an opportunity for publicity pass him by, issued a "style show" challenge to the White Sox, inviting newspaper society editors to cover a scheduled doubleheader between the clubs in May.

Skipper Al Lopez modeled the new look in mid-March, noting that his predecessor Jimmie Dykes "probably will blow a kiss to me when he sees this getup."

While the expected pithy comments inevitably arrived, some enlightened observers deemed the uniforms to be attractive. The move was even hailed by the tradition-bound *Sporting News*, which called the White Sox' look "progressive." "After all," they wrote, "road uniforms DON'T HAVE to be gray."

Chicago pushed all their powder blue chips forward into the middle of the table two years later, experimenting with caps that matched the uniforms, but these were forsaken after just a handful of appearances.

The Sox abandoned powder blue for boring gray in 1969, but just as the Athletics passed them the torch, they in turn passed it along to two brand new expansion clubs, the Seattle Pilots and the Montreal Expos.

Neil Armstrong made "one giant leap for mankind" when he stepped onto the surface of the moon, the war in Vietnam slogged forward, and the Mets—THE METS!—won the World Series. As the sixties lapsed into the seventies, tastes changed, and, in 1972, sales of color televisions finally surpassed those of black-and-white sets.

The Philadelphia Phillies' new powder blues were so popular that they petitioned the National League to let them wear them for all games, both home and away. Pitcher Dick Selma lobbied for the move, and he had the support of his teammates and manager. The club wore them at home just once, on June 10 against Atlanta, but decided to shelve the plan in favor of the conventional setup.

The *Philadelphia Inquirer* termed them "the fashion hit of the 1972 season . . . a vast improvement on the traditional drab grays."

The Chicago Cubs took the concept of powder blue uniforms and catapulted it into a whole new place in 1978, when they adopted new road uniforms that some likened to pajamas. They were a trendy powder blue, a hue that the club had worn while traveling for several years at this point, but they made use of white pinstripes, a look that was less than flattering.

By 1980, eleven of baseball's twenty-six teams would be clad in powder blue. That year the Phillies and Royals matched up in the World Series, the first in which both league champions wore powder blue on the road. Two years later, the St. Louis Cardinals and Milwaukee Brewers followed suit with St. Louis, an old-school team by anyone's definition, winning it all in their "victory blues."

The trend began to recede toward the end of the eighties. Core powder blue clubs such as Minnesota, Philadelphia, and Milwaukee went back to boring old gray while traveling, and by 1991 the Montreal Expos stood alone as the last holdouts.

* * *

When it comes to colorful uniforms, a little bit can go a long way—but too much can really be *too much*.

Take the Baltimore Orioles, for instance.

On September 16, 1971, the Baltimore Orioles were kings of baseball: the defending World Series Champions, a perennial powerhouse, and a team on the cusp of yet another American League pennant.

Halloween came early that night when the Orioles took the field clad in all-orange, a dramatic chromatic contrast to their opponents that evening, the New York Yankees, garbed in drab gray flannel.

The jerseys featured the Orioles' usual script lettering, rendered in black with a white outline and a large, 5-inch number underneath. Four gigantic sleeve stripes served as a ballast. They were constructed using form-fitting double knit fabric, a new innovation that had been introduced by the Pittsburgh Pirates the previous year.

The pants completed the overall picture: all orange with thinner black and white stripes running down the sides.

The look was met with instant ridicule. Pitcher Dave McNally said, "I just wish that the guys who ordered these would have to wear them." The hometown *Baltimore Sun* called them "four shades more lustrous than a ripe autumn pumpkin."

Not everyone disapproved, however. "I like 'em," quipped utility infielder Chico Salmon, a native of Panama. "They bring out the blackness in me."

The uniforms were supplied by the Brooks Robinson Sporting Goods Company, co-owned by the Orioles' Hall of Fame third baseman. Robinson hit a grand slam in the eighth inning the night they were first worn against the Yankees, thus becoming the first player in major-league history to drive in four runs with one swing while dressed as a traffic cone.

The plan was to wear them both at home and on the road for the remainder of the regular season, but the uniforms only saw the light of day a few more times, finally meeting their maker the following April in a game against Cleveland.

But, like something out of a horror movie, the orange togs refused to die. In 1973, they were resurrected by the Orioles' Florida State League single-A affiliate in Miami. The "M-Orioles" manager, Bobby Malkmus, wearing Dave McNally's old orange number 19 outfit, told the *Miami News* that his guys liked them and that they were "just happy to be wearing any color uniform." The *News* noted "(t)he manager said his dugout seemed 10 degrees warmer on opening night because of the infrared glow . . . cast by the bright uniforms."

Brooks Robinson may have broken new ground with his grand slam, but John Wesley "Boog" Powell owns the distinction of having worn uniforms that conjured up thoughts of both a traffic cone AND an enormous candied apple.

Powell was a big man. He clocked in at a robust 6-foot-4 and weighed about 230 pounds at the time of the 1975 trade that sent him from Baltimore to the Cleveland Indians.

That season, Cleveland upped their uniform game in a big way, adding an all-red ensemble that made its debut on Opening Day.

Red is a powerful color. A pullover red jersey, red beltless pants, and red stirrups combine to make a loud, powerful statement. The look was destined to draw attention, even before it was ever worn in an actual game.

Prior to the 1975 season, thirty-seven Cleveland players signed a petition, addressed to club president Ted Bonda, asking that the Tribe add a navy blue jersey to their ensemble.

An Associated Press story reported, "one player who confirmed that the request had been made said those who signed the petition were offering to buy the blue tops themselves if the Indian brass won't spend $30 a shirt for the change in the sartorial scheme." They eventually got them.

Cleveland manager Frank Robinson cut a graceful presence in every uniform he ever wore. Outfielder Oscar Gamble owned the most epic afro in the history of Major League Baseball—this served as a distraction from the chromatic impact of his all-red uniforms.

But Powell, a conspicuous presence, could not hide.

"That's the biggest Bloody Mary I ever saw," quipped Mark Belanger, Powell's former Orioles teammate. Powell himself observed, "I felt like a massive blood clot."

On Saturday night, May 19, 1979, the Philadelphia Phillies rolled out their new all-burgundy uniforms—a look that consisted of burgundy tops and pants, burgundy belts, caps, undershirts, and stirrups. And burgundy shoes. That evening the Phillies, a visage in maroon, juxtaposed against the flat green artificial surface of Veteran's Stadium, managed to make the all-red Indians look like fashion icons.

The plan was for the team to wear them every Saturday, both at home and on the road, but reaction was both swift and harsh. Matters were made worse by the fact that the uniforms didn't fit right, running way too big for players' tastes. Phils slugger Greg Luzinski, a large man who was nicknamed "The Bull," complained that his jersey extended below his knees.

They photographed poorly, too. Newspaper photos, shot and printed in black and white in those days, picked up player faces and the broad white stripes that ran down the sides of the uniforms, but not much else.

As if all that were not enough, pitcher Dick Ruthven's jersey was misspelt as "Ruthben."

The Phillies scrapped the uniforms after that single game and announced a week later that they would be selling them to the public for $200 each, with proceeds going to charity.

* * *

The nineties gave us many things, including Beanie Babies, light-up sneakers, and AOL screen names. The nineties also brought forth a slew of alternate jerseys, some of which contained the defining pro sports colors of the decade—teal, silver, black, and purple. The 1993 season ushered in new franchises in Miami (black, teal, and silver) and Denver (black, purple, and silver). Five years later, Arizona (black, purple, a greenish teal, and copper) and Tampa Bay (black and purple, along with a secondary cast of characters) joined the majors.

The origins of this trend-driven phenomenon can be attributed to the wildly successful launch of the NBA's Charlotte Hornets brand in 1988. The previous year, fashion designer Alexander Julian was hired to design uniforms for the expansion Hornets. His designs captured the imagination of the American sports world. If ever there was a tipping point that brought American fashion and American sports together, this was it.

While baseball's chromatic palette expanded in new directions during the waning years of the twentieth century, the color was confined to the tops of the uniforms, in the form of alternate jerseys. Pants, for the most part, remained either white or gray, and they grew longer, thus obscuring the time-honored stirrups that helped add color to the bottoms of the overall uniform since the days of the Cincinnati Red Stockings.

Fortune, it has been said, favors the bold. Let us give praise to the rainbow-colored bounty that Charlie Finley, Boog Powell, Oscar Gamble, and the 1998 Tampa Bay Devil Rays have bequeathed to us. We are better off for it, even if part of that contribution involves Bloody Marys, ripe autumn pumpkins, and blood clots.

The 1901 Baltimore Orioles sported gaudy road uniforms of black and yellow. These were likely the brainchild of player/manager John McGraw, an enthusiastic uniform buff who trotted his 1905 and 1911 New York Giants World Series squads out in similarly dark togs.

The below news item provides a vivid description of "Muggsy's" creation, a look that stood out at a time when color was rapidly disappearing from the field of play across the majors. Baltimore wore these uniforms for but a single season before switching to boring, conventional grays for the franchise's final campaign the following year.

Charley Dryden of the Philadelphia North American staff thus describes the Oriole uniforms: "We don't know whether Muggsy designed them himself or engaged a cake walker to twist his intellect on the job. From the knees down the Orioles look as if they had waded in raw omelet, which adhered in streaks. The yellow legs fade away into two black bags, supported by a yellow belt. Then comes a black shirt, with an immense yellow O on the left breast. Over this harmonious whole is worn a double-breasted coat, with wide yellow collar and cuffs of the same, and two rows of white pearl buttons as large as oyster shells down the front breadths. All that is needed to complete the ensemble of the hottest bunch in Dixie is a pink plug hat. If Muggsy wishes to add the hat he is welcome to this tip."

THE EVENING STAR, THURSDAY, MAY 9, 1901.

The 1975 Cleveland Indians finished in fourth place, but their legacy is secure, thanks to a couple of very memorable things. One would be "Ten Cent Beer Night," an ill-conceived promotion that they hosted in June. It resulted in exactly what you'd think it would. Also of note was the Tribe's new red alternate jersey, which, when paired with red pants the following year, caused Boog Powell to liken himself to "a massive blood clot."

The result was conspicuous enough to warrant thirty-seven players to petition team ownership, demanding relief in the form of alternate navy blue jerseys.

The Kansas City Athletics' green and gold uniforms rocked the colorless world of baseball when they were introduced in 1963. Though widely derided at the time, they served as the first volley in the Technicolor revolution that soon followed.

Baseball history is chock full of pinstriped uniforms, and it's usually an understated and classy design feature. The Chicago Cubs, however, decided to make every road game one big pajama party with these togs, which were worn from 1978–81.

May 19, 1979, represents a critically important date in the history of the ugly baseball uniform. It was on this night at Philadelphia's Veterans Stadium that the hometown Phillies took the field clad all in burgundy from head to toe, a singularly '70s visage if ever there was one.

The club intended to feature the uniforms as a regular alternate set, but they scrapped these plans after that single game, a sartorial experiment gone horribly wrong. One can question the optics of the whole thing, and indeed, that was part of the issue. When photographed, the uniforms afforded a pronounced lack of contrast, an especially important thing considering the fact that newspapers back then were printed in black and white. They were also sized incorrectly, thus earning the enmity of many of the Phillies' players, including pitcher Dick Ruthven, whose jersey read "Ruthben."

For the first two decades of their existence the San Diego Padres were conspicuously clad in brown and yellow. While some fans see a unique franchise palette, others look at the colors and think of UPS.

Of the brown, San Diego infielder Kurt Bevacqua once remarked, "We look like nine piles of manure in a cow pasture." Shortly after Steve Garvey shifted from the Los Angeles Dodgers to San Diego he told *Sports Illustrated*, "I used to look like an American flag. The Padre uniform makes me look like a taco."

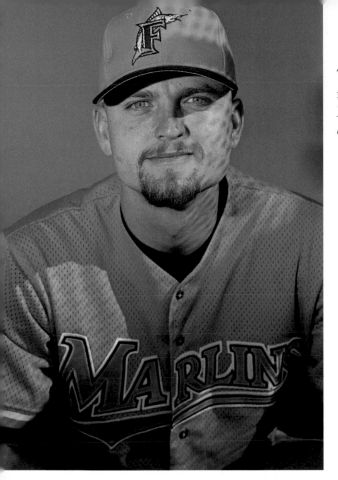

The Florida Marlins introduced teal into MLB's family of colors in 1993, modeled here by future San Diego Padres icon Trevor Hoffman. The Marlins' aqua/teal color, officially designated "Marlins blue," tracked trends of the era but seemed perfectly at home in post–*Miami Vice* South Florida.

The Texas Rangers bucked tradition when they introduced a new uniform set in 1984. The Rangers wore standard whites at home, but they eliminated gray while on the road in favor of blue and red jerseys, all of which were paired with white pants.

Arizona joined the National League in 1998, garbed in a slew of different uniform options, including this purple number. This jersey contains several '90s-a-riffic uniform elements—purple and turquoise? Check. Black? Aye, captain. Metallic copper trim, multiple outlines, and a black drop shadow complete the picture.

Buck Showalter took the reins of the Arizona Diamondbacks on November 15, 1995, nearly two and a half years before they played their first official game. The club's inaugural look featured these off-white caps, which, when paired with purple, black, turquoise, and copper, made for a truly '90s visage.

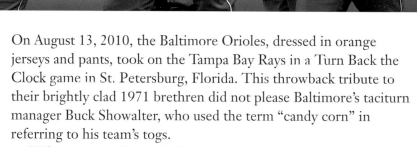

On August 13, 2010, the Baltimore Orioles, dressed in orange jerseys and pants, took on the Tampa Bay Rays in a Turn Back the Clock game in St. Petersburg, Florida. This throwback tribute to their brightly clad 1971 brethren did not please Baltimore's taciturn manager Buck Showalter, who used the term "candy corn" in referring to his team's togs.

"Take a picture," he said, "because you won't see them again."

INNING 3

RAINBOW GUTS, SHORTS, BEACH BLANKETS, AND BUMBLEBEES

Rainbow Guts, Shorts, Beach Blankets, and Bumblebees

Perched high atop Mount Polyester, there lies a Pantheon of ugly uniforms.

It is time.

The time has come to talk about the most distinctive, recognizable uniforms in the long history of Major League Baseball.

When they made their debut one observer opined that it looked like the players' vital organs were on fire. Another compared the athletes to large orange popsicles.

April 7, 1975, was the date that the ugly baseball uniform achieved its apotheosis. That evening at the Houston Astrodome, the Astros took the field for their season opener against the Atlanta Braves, outfitted in pullover uniforms that were officially described by the National League as having "yellow, orange, and burnt orange stripes on body and sleeves."

As if the team needed any further form of identification, the word "Astros," rendered in navy blue contemporary sans-serif letterforms, sat atop the stripes. And there, on the player's bellies, sat a huge 9 1/8-inch-high Texas star.

Beltless pants helped complete the ensemble, featuring a gigantic red waistband and thick red, orange, light orange, and yellow stripes running horizontally down the sides. As if to complete the picture, player numbers were placed on the upper right thighs, a major-league first.

Just wait—there's more. The backs of the jerseys that first season incorporated a huge white circle that contained player numbers, rendered in a circus-inspired font.

The tequila sunrises. The rainbows. The rainbow GUTS. A legend was born that night in the always comfortable, air-conditioned Astrodome, thus setting the gold standard for what a wonderfully ugly baseball uniform could look like.

Just how unique was this getup? It was so singularly uncommon that the club wore the same outfits at home and on the road, for all games, a breach of uniform protocol that few even noticed.

Astros owner Judge Roy Hofheinz was a man who thought big. He earned his law degree at the age of nineteen, and later became a two-term mayor of Houston. He had a plan to defeat nature itself and made it happen, conceiving of and building the world's first indoor domed sports stadium, referred to by many as the Eighth Wonder of the World, the Astrodome.

Of his team's new uniforms, Hofheinz said, "I take a major part in damn near everything around here, good, bad, or indifferent." Which was an indirect way of saying that the buck stopped there, even if he wasn't directly responsible for them.

Longtime Astros executive Tal Smith says that Sidney Shlenker, executive vice president of Astrodomain, by then the holding company that controlled the ball club, was the man who spearheaded the uniform refresh and oversaw the whole process.

This makes sense. Like Hofheinz, Shlenker was a promotional juggernaut, notably putting together and staging the "Battle of the Sexes" tennis match between Billie Jean King and Bobby Riggs, staged at the Astrodome in September 1973.

The club brought in heavy-hitter ad agency McCann-Erickson to give the Astros a makeover, a revolutionary move in and of itself in an age where such things were usually left to the Rawlings and Spaldings of the world.

A couple of blurry photos reveal a prototype. They depict pitcher Tom Griffin, staring straight ahead, a posed look on his face—perhaps he is stifling a laugh? He is standing in front of a white backdrop that doesn't quite reach the floor. The lighting is harsh, the whole thing resembles a scene from some focus group holding cell where a mug shot is being taken.

A white cap with an italicized letter "A," a white star within, tops his head flanked on the left by a series of warmly colored stripes. The soon to be familiar rainbow guts are there, but there's a massive WHITE star—Judge Hofheinz later said that it was scrapped for dark blue "so as not to hide a pitch."

Incongruously, Griffin is wearing dark-colored stirrups, topped by two simple bands of orange. They seem like an anachronism, a misplaced throwback to some distant age, a tipoff to the fact that this "Man of the Future" is actually a time traveler being fitted for his time travel suit. He is a man who looks like he is being readied by some secret crack NASA team for his mission. He is *Major Tom*

Griffin, about to check ignition, ready to propel the Astros into a galaxy far distant from any other MLB club.

Once they hit the field, reactions were mixed. Charles O. Finley's green and gold A's, now located in Oakland, were back-to-back-to-back World Series Champions, an association that gave luster to what were considered garish clown outfits a dozen years earlier. Some observers praised the innovative nature of the look, while others inevitably scoffed. Los Angeles Dodgers pitcher Charlie Hough, for instance, said "they look like Hawaiian softball uniforms."

The Astros introduced a tame, conventional gray road uniform in 1980, one that relegated the rainbow stripes to the sleeves, then discarded the signature rainbow guts entirely after the historic 1986 National League Championship Series, in which Houston lost to the New York Mets.

The rainbow-striped sleeves hung around through the 1993 season, like a vestigial remnant of some distant, defeated empire. Then . . . poof! Just like that, the Astros became just another team, handsome but boring in their midnight navy blue and gold duds with the aggressively pointy open star logo.

I am reminded of actor Ray Liotta's line in the last scene of the classic mob movie *Goodfellas*. After a fast-paced, interesting, glamorous life of crime, he is exiled to live out his days as a resident of some soulless suburban cul-de-sac, lamenting the fact that he was now "an average nobody . . . get to live the rest of my life like a schnook."

More than three decades after they were left behind, what exactly is the enduring appeal of the Astros' rainbow look?

For one thing, they represent the ultimate example of baseball's march forward, toward a modern on-field aesthetic. They look like nothing that came before—or since. For me, one look at these uniforms continues to reveal a sense of warmth and happiness—humanity even—an exuberant chromatic affirmation of the fact that BASEBALL IS SPORTS AND SPORTS ARE FUN!

Mike Acosta, a Houston native, is the Astros authentication manager and the team's in-house historian. He says, "the look of the rainbow uniform is just simply . . . Houston. People know exactly what it is when they see those stripes. Older generations have introduced their younger kids to this look and while it might not exactly mean the same thing to these kids, it's just like any other tradition in baseball that's passed down over the years.

"The star with the inset 'H' and the rainbow stripes are synonymous with this city. It's a link to the past and present. I can recall when the Astros were referred to as a young franchise, but it's now fifty-five years since the Colt .45s debuted and over forty years since the rainbows came around, and people still identify with them.

"It's definitely civic pride," he says. "Houston is a very diverse, international city and has been for a long time. By working for the team over the past nineteen seasons I have come to know and meet many Astros fans who come from very different backgrounds and are all fueled by their passion for this team. I recall myself as a kid wearing the rainbow uniform to school and sometimes being made fun of by other kids because the Astros were having a losing season. I guess I always just saw it as having pride in something and sticking with it. It's nice to see that these colors have grown into a symbol of pride, almost like a landmark."

Powered by the warm glow of nostalgia, the tequila sunrises harken back to a less dogmatic, more spontaneous time. It's Houston in the late seventies, hoss. Grab yourself a Lone Star longneck, set a while in the Eighth Wonder of the World, cooled to a comfortably constant 72 degrees, and watch some dang baseball.

Incidentally, the connection between the term "tequila sunrise" and the Astros uniforms seems to have originated with Florida sportswriter Shelby Strother, who first made the association in 1979. Among all the things the uniforms have ever been called, this one may well be the most enduring.

The Astros roll out the rainbows as throwbacks on a regular basis, and they are always a hit with fans. Their 2013 visual refresh even made sure to incorporate the horizontal rainbow stripes on the sides of their batting practice jerseys, a nod to both history and public opinion.

If the Astros' rainbow outfits are the most enduringly beloved on-field identity of the golden era of the ugly baseball uniform, then the Chicago White Sox' 1976 redesign is firmly embedded in our collective consciousness as its most bizarre and, probably, most memorable.

Contemporary readers who are even remotely familiar with the White Sox' uniforms of the late seventies and early eighties will knowingly smirk, recalling the fact that these South Side Sox were the ones who wore shorts.

They did. For a grand total of *four games*, all played during the month of August, 1976. That's it. The first time they went bare-kneed was on August 8 of that year, against Kansas City.[1] The Sox then wore

---

1   The White Sox broke out their shorts for the first game of a doubleheader against Kansas City, changing into their usual uniforms for game two.

the shorts three times against the Orioles: on August 21, and for both games of a doubleheader the following day.

White Sox' owner Bill Veeck's audacious experiment was so utterly strange that, more than four decades later, we know all about the shorts, even though they were worn for a mere thirty-nine innings, total.

It's perfectly fitting that Veeck is the individual connected to the weirdest MLB uniform of all time. Veeck's Hall of Fame plaque cites his "ingenious promotional schemes," and references the fact that he was the man who first put player names on the backs of big-league uniforms, in 1960. He was also famous for thumbing his nose at convention, as well as at his fellow team owners.

In December 1975, Veeck led a group that purchased the White Sox, then a stagnant franchise in deep trouble (having enjoyed just one winning season from 1968–74). The moribund Sox were nearly purchased by a Seattle group who would have shifted the whole operation to the Pacific Northwest, but Veeck and company stepped in to save the team for Chicago. Veeck's standing among White Sox fans was solid—he previously owned the club from 1959–61, a short tenure that delivered an American League pennant that first year.

This was clearly a situation in dire need of Bill Veeck's legendary talents. Veeck was a man who knew and understood the power of visuals, having cut his teeth under his father, who served as president of the crosstown Cubs from 1919 until his death in 1933. The younger Veeck embraced the idea of uniforms as a marketing tool during his stints as owner of the Cleveland Indians, where he introduced Chief Wahoo in 1947, and in St. Louis, where he ran the Browns.

The uniforms that he commissioned for the 1976 White Sox would not disappoint.

In early February, news reports indicated that Veeck was considering outfitting the Sox as "track stars." The Associated Press said that Veeck was "polling designers and manufacturers to find a uniform that will project a new image." He hinted that shorts were under consideration, but seemingly hedged his bets by stating, "I don't want to make them wear shorts under duress."

What emerged at a March 9 press conference/fashion show was truly odd and noteworthy, an attention-grab of Veeckian proportions. The uniforms, modeled by five former White Sox players, *did* feature shorts as one option, but that was but a single strange element among many weird aspects of the Sox' new on-field look. Veeck's wife, Mary Frances, reportedly designed them.

How about "clamdiggers," or knee-length pants? And un-tucked, floppy-collared shirts? It was the shorts, however, that stole the show, advertised as a hot-weather option and referred to as "Hollywood shorts," a tribute to similar gear worn by the minor-league Hollywood Stars back in the 1950s.

"Players should not worry about their vanity, but their comfort. If it's 95 degrees out, an athlete should be glad to put on short pants and forget his bony knees," said Veeck. "Hell, I've got a worse looking knee than any of my players. It's solid wood." (A World War II injury during his stint in the Marine Corps cost Veeck most of his right leg.)

First baseman/designated hitter Lamar Johnson seemed to like them. "I got the nicest thighs you ever saw," he said. "I can't wait." On the other hand, Catcher Jim Essian said, "I'll just shave my legs. When we slide in those things and get all cut up, we'll need to shave before we put the bandages on anyway, right?"

For all the unusual aspects of these now-legendary outfits, the graphics were decidedly sedate and traditional. Navy blue and white Tuscan-style lettering, similar to that worn by the Boston Red Sox, called out the word "Chicago" across the fronts of both home and road jerseys, with similarly old-fashioned numbers and letters spelling out the players' names and numbers on the backs.

Veeck was inspired by his franchise's earliest look, one that he said was "a flashback . . . but a flashback to class." Actual white socks were also part of the mix, a fitting accouterment for a team called "White Sox."

Naturally, reaction was sharp and snarky. One *Los Angeles Times* writer opined that "the White Sox wear uniforms that make them look like the softball team at the fat man's picnic." Fiery New York Yankees manager Billy Martin said that the Sox' white sleeves, paired with their navy blue road uniforms, violated the rules of baseball. Comparing the Sox' funky togs to the tastefully refined Yankees' pinstripes, Martin noted "our uniforms were designed by men."

My personal memories of that White Sox uniform are most vividly focused on the Yankees' home opener in the Bronx, on April 13, 1978. I was one of 44,667 lucky fans who

watched portly White Sox knuckleballer Wilbur Wood, pitching in his final major-league season, cough up a three-run homer to Reggie Jackson in the first inning. Jackson had hit three consecutive homers in the final game of the previous World Series, also played at the Stadium, and the crowd went berserk.

The Yankees handed out "Reggie!" candy bars to all who attended the opener that day, and when their namesake blasted Wood's flat 2–0 knuckleball over the 385-foot sign in right-center field, the Bronx sky was suddenly transformed into a flying blitzkrieg of milk chocolate, peanut butter, and roasted peanuts, sheathed in bright orange wrappers.

The game was halted for five minutes as the White Sox stood by, despondent and more than a little worried, garbed in their silly uniforms. Someone could have been hurt, said Chicago skipper Bob Lemon. "People starving all over the world, and 30 billion calories are laying on the field."

I ate the candy bar, but I still have the ticket stub from that day.

These were the uniforms that witnessed "Disco Demolition Night," the White Sox' 1979 promotion-gone-wrong that provoked a full-scale riot and helped usher out the century's weirdest decade on an appropriately weird note. The following year, liberal peanut-farmer-turned-politician Jimmy Carter was evicted from 1600 Pennsylvania Avenue in favor of conservative actor-turned-politician Ronald Reagan and, as America awaited the Gipper's inauguration, the White Sox' ownership again changed hands.

Perpetually short on cash (if not ideas), Bill Veeck and his ownership group sold the franchise to Eddie Einhorn and Jerry Reinsdorf in January 1981. In their maiden press conference, the new owners declared that changes would be made, specifically referencing the Sox' uniforms.[2]

---

2   The Veeck uniforms did enjoy one more brief flirtation with infamy decades later, when they were to be used as throwbacks in a June 2016 game against the Tigers. Rather than wear them, Chicago ace lefty Chris Sale cut up his uniform, along with those of his teammates, drawing a five-game suspension.

In April 1981, the White Sox announced a "Dress Your Own Team" contest to redesign the much-maligned "leisure suit" look. More than 1,500 designs were submitted; these were narrowed down to six finalists a few months later.

The six contenders represented a drastic break toward a more contemporary aesthetic. All of them were full of stripes—vertical stripes down the sleeves and pants, horizontal stripes across chests and bellies, and one that featured gigantic red and blue stripes that slithered from the neckline down to the opposing sleeve like a big fat boa constrictor. Another was a blatant rip-off of the Astros' signature look, with horizontal blocks of color across the gut, fronted by—wow, how original!—a mammoth five-pointed star.

Player reaction to the six proposed replacements was less than enthusiastic, regardless of what they were replacing. When the results of fan voting were announced, uniform design number two was the winner, a creation that, with some changes, became the White Sox uniform for the next five seasons.

The final product, designed by twenty-six-year-old Richard Launius, was unveiled in March 1982. The central feature of the jerseys was a 4 1/8-inch tall navy blue band, sandwiched between 7/8-inch red bands, with the word SOX centered between. Red player numbers 4 inches high were placed on the pants, which were topped off by a generously proportioned navy blue waistband.

Chicago Tribune columnist Steve Daley summed it all up when he wrote, "The old uniforms made the Sox look like an industrial softball team in Moline," but the new ones made Greg Luzinski, the Sox' large designated hitter, look "like a box of cereal or a road sign."

Some very good players filled out these uniforms, including Hall of Famers Carlton Fisk, Tom Seaver, and, for ten games in 1986, Steve Carlton.

The 1983 White Sox won the American League West, and their team slogan was "Winning Ugly," although that had more to do with their playing style than their uniforms (although it all made sense). Texas Rangers manager Doug Rader, who, having played for the 1975 Astros and knew a little something about ugly uniforms, coined the phrase.

*   *   *

No discussion of the golden era of the ugly baseball uniform would be complete without mention of the Pittsburgh Pirates' mix-and-match outfits that they wore from 1977–84. The Bucs were already uniform trailblazers, having broken new ground in 1970 when they became the first MLB club to wear truly revolutionary synthetic uniforms, devoid of belts and buttons.

In 1976, the club adopted flat-topped "Anson-style" caps in honor of the National League's 100th anniversary celebration. While several NL clubs also wore the retro headwear that season, the Pirates wore them for every single game. The initial plan was to go back to the usual hats for 1977, but fate obviously intervened, because the Pirates came back that year with a uniform set that seemed to perfectly complement their weird retro chapeaus.

On page 58 of the 1977 Pittsburgh Pirates yearbook, there is a full-bleed photo, taken on a sunny day at the Bucs' spring training facility in Bradenton, Florida. Manager Chuck Tanner stands at center, smiling and cradling a baseball. He is wearing a yellow/gold flat-topped hat with three black stripes. His uniform is also striped, but these are not just any old pinstripes. These are gold, with black on either side, a unique triple-stripe that serves as ballast for his golden sleeves and stirrups. Big sleeve and neck stripes complete the look.

On his right is Bill Robinson, the Pirates' versatile veteran hitter, looking like a 6-foot-2-inch-tall banana. His cap, jersey, and pants are all gold, his stirrups and sleeves are black.

Standing on Tanner's left is Buc pitcher Jim Rooker, hands on hips, doing his best Johnny Cash impersonation. This man in black, however, has golden sleeves and stirrups, just like his manager, and he has a broad smile on his face, probably secure in the knowledge that the other two guys drew the short straw when it came to deciding who would wear what getup.

All three uniforms were interchangeable, which made for a total of nine different combinations. Toss in the two different caps, two different undershirts, and two different colored sets of stirrups and it suddenly becomes clear that the Pirates' equipment manager had his work cut out for him.

The team courted controversy by purchasing the pinstriped uniforms from a Japanese company, a point of great contention in 1977 Pittsburgh, a city whose steel industry was teetering on the precipice of what would soon be an historic collapse. Club officials defended the move, saying that American suppliers couldn't manufacture what they were looking for.

Pitcher Jerry Reuss won 220 games across 22 major-league seasons. A native of St. Louis, he began his career with the Cardinals, garbed in their timelessly classic uniform, a look that he calls "impressive."

Reuss's professional journey took him to eight big-league teams, including the Pirates, where he starred from 1974–78. His memories of the club's mix-and-match uniforms are vivid and filled with strong aesthetic opinions. Reuss is an accomplished photographer and a man with a keen eye for uniforms and for the visual culture of the sport.

I loved the Pirates first set of double-knit uniforms. That understated look of old gold and black had just the right balance of color and design to make the look unique and stylish. In 1976, when the club changed to the pillbox hat, I believe the move altered the dynamic of the design and made the uniform look like a gimmick.

In Spring Training of 1977, I saw the new sets of uniforms that we would wear that year. Gone was the understated look. My first thought was someone went to a Steelers game, liked the way the black top/gold pants combination appeared on the field we shared with the Steelers (Three Rivers Stadium), and thought, "We can take this look light years from here." Thus, the mix-and-match combo idea. No team used this concept previously, and the new Pirate front office management wanted to forge their new path with the new uniform style leading the way.

For me, the all-black uniform was a non-starter. It was too hot to wear on artificial turf fields in the summer and the television cameras had a difficult time showing the faces of some of our players on night telecasts.

The pinstriped uniform was too busy, with a vertical yellow stripe sandwiched with thinner black stripes. The bolder three-striped trim on the neck, sleeves, and waistband in a horizontal direction, the black wordmark with yellow trim and the striped pillbox hats made this oversaturated combination of stripes in every direction simply overbearing.

The solid yellow was the best looking of the three, especially when viewed from the seats as it played well against the green of the turf or grass, the contrasting color of the stadium walls and the blue sky. The black and white trim on the uniform top and pants gave the uniform definition and was easiest on the eyes.

None of the combinations worked for me. Mixing the pinstripes with a solid color threw any selection out of balance without any proportion. The solid combos solved the balance problem but did nothing about the aesthetics. Black pants for a baseball uniform are never a good choice. Seeing pictures of those combos today make it seem as if we dressed in the dark!

Reuss's memories of the Pirates' signature pillbox caps are less than kind. "I didn't like the pillbox hats then and still don't like the look of them today. Many Pirate fans disagreed with my opinion. The black pillbox with three gold horizontal stripes was a top seller among concession items for years. It's just a matter of opinion."

Regardless of what the uniforms looked like, Reuss notes, he wore them with pride. "Once I was blessed to wear a major-league uniform, I made it a point to look at myself in the mirror every day before I entered the field to make sure that I dressed with that same pride and dignity. After all, I was living my dream."

The 1977 Pirates opened the regular season at home against the Cardinals, dressed in black and gold pinstripes from head to toe—Jerry Reuss holds the distinction of having been the Bucs' Opening Day starting pitcher. The next game was an all-gold affair, and the following game saw the Bucs dressed all in black. St. Louis swept the three-game series, and a change was clearly in order. The Pirates got their first win of the young season against Montreal two days later, clad in gold tops and black pants.

The Bucs of these years were a team on the move, and their flamboyant uniforms were a signature component of the most colorful matchup in Fall Classic history, a fitting conclusion to the game's most colorful decade.

The night of Wednesday, October 10, 1979, forever changed the trajectory of my young life, for it was on this evening that the Pittsburgh Pirates faced off against the Baltimore Orioles in Game One of the 76th World Series, live and in vivid, screaming, vibrant color, broadcast on the ABC television network.

At approximately 8:30 EST, my nearsighted fifteen-year-old retinas were singed as Omar Moreno, the Pirates' speedy center fielder, clad in a black jersey and gold pants, stepped to the plate to face Baltimore lefty Mike Flanagan, resplendent in his bright orange jersey and white pants.

While the entire decade of the seventies was a colorful affair for baseball, this was the *World Series*. Yes, the Oakland A's won three straight championships in green and gold several years earlier, but they did so against three teams that followed baseball's timeless visual traditions: the Reds, Mets, and Dodgers. The 1975 Series was a classic, Boston versus Cincinnati, but it was also a colorless one, as were the next three, with the Reds, Dodgers, and Yankees dressed in home whites and road grays.

I have been to the Pantheon in Rome, an ancient structure whose interior is considered by many to be the most aesthetically perfect space in all the world. Our Pantheon of ugly uniforms is anything but perfect, but it is both memorable and worthy of discussion—a sacred place where rainbows fill the sky and polyester leisure suits are eternally stylish.

In 1978, Pittsburgh captain Willie Stargell started awarding embroidered stars to teammates for on-field contributions, both big and small. The stars were affixed to the Pirates' signature pillbox caps and were catapulted into the public consciousness a year later when the Bucs won the World Series.

The Chicago White Sox' 1976 dalliance with shorts makes a strong claim to be the single weirdest major-league uniform of all time.

Sox players' public comments were diplomatic, but their opponents pulled no punches. "You guys are the sweetest team we've seen yet," chirped Royals first baseman John Mayberry.

Oakland A's owner Charlie Finley, himself a uniform innovator worthy of Hall of Fame status, dissed the look in saying "there's nothing worse than looking at a man's legs . . . I've yet to meet a woman who likes the average man's legs, although I like to wear shorts and think I have nice legs. Bill Veeck's team doesn't."

While the White Sox' connection with shorts is indelibly embedded in our collective memories, they were only worn a total of four times, all in the month of August.

Major League Baseball's *Official Uniform and Specifications Guide* described them as such: "Curved bottom (worn outside of pants) pullover style shirt with open, navy blue v-neck front; Half Byron collar (collar on front only)." (Also, Andre the Giant perfected the Half Byron in a 1980 match against Hulk Hogan, but I digress.)

Of the un-tucked jerseys, legendary columnist Jim Murray wrote, "They make everybody look fat. They put Greg Luzinski on the cover of a magazine in a Chicago White Sox uniforms the other day and set the sport back about 90 years."

Some observers saw beach blankets while others saw license plates. I am, of course, speaking of the uniforms of the mid-'80s Chicago White Sox, a first ballot inductee into the Wonderfully Ugly Baseball Uniform Hall of Fame.

Gigantic blocks of color and chunky graphics help make this a classic among classics. Numbers on the players' pants inject a touch of weirdness into the mix for an unforgettable look.

They are the most distinctive uniforms in the long history of Major League Baseball. Call them what you want—rainbows, rainbow guts, tequila sunrises, whatever—this jersey is the single greatest representation of baseball's 1972–86 pivot away from its longstanding sartorial traditions.

This particular example dates to 1982. There are some wonderful details to take note of here, starting with the "Astros" lettering. Note that it is off-center, intentionally shifted toward the right side of the jersey. This allows the "s" and the "t" to perfectly bisect the bottom point of the navy blue v-neck trim.

The colossal Texas-sized star is outlined in white here, but it was bordered in red from the time of the uniforms' introduction in 1975 up until 1981.

The signature stripes are rendered in two different oranges, yellow, and red, all fused together in an audacious display that will never be confused with any other uniform, before or since.

Houston killed off their tequila sunrise jerseys in 1986, but they have enjoyed an active afterlife, warmly embraced by a generation of fans who have no firsthand knowledge of just how radical they were when originally launched.

The Astros first revived them as part of their final season in the Astrodome, in 1999. Closer Billy Wagner called them "clown suits." (Photo courtesy of the author)

INNING

4

THE GOLDEN ERA
OF UGLY UNIFORMS

The Golden Era of Ugly Uniforms

I will go on record right now in saying that the golden era of the ugly baseball uniform spanned the years 1972 to 1986.

Why did this particular moment in time deliver the most vibrant, most interesting (and sometimes the most awful) uniforms that the sport has ever seen?

Let's start at the beginning of that stretch.

When the Pittsburgh Pirates took the field outfitted in pullover jerseys and beltless pants on July 16, 1970, they expanded upon Charlie Finley's revolutionary turn away from the traditional definition of what a baseball uniform looked like.

Pullover jerseys allowed for a more expansive piece of real estate on which to display graphics, previously constricted by the traditional buttons that effectively served as a roadblock, often slicing team lettering into discrete halves.

The Bucs utilized the elasticized waistbands on their pants as a vessel for color, replacing the usual belt with a series of three wide horizontal stripes that provided an additional opportunity for brand extension that had never before existed in baseball.

Fashion in the early seventies was, of course, a hideous disaster when viewed through our contemporary lens, but the golden era of the ugly baseball uniform is firmly rooted in the era of polyester leisure suits, low-rise bell bottoms, and platform shoes.

When the Atlanta Braves unveiled the streamlined royal blue and white look that Hank Aaron would later wear when he broke Babe Ruth's career home-run record. Braves manager Luman Harris had only words of praise.

"Mod's the word these days as far as baseball players are concerned," said Harris. "If people think these new uniforms are something, they ought to see [how the players dress] after the game . . . I wear colored shirts now that I wouldn't have been caught dead in five years ago."

He was, of course, right.

Take a look at a newspaper from the summer of 1972. There, amidst distressing news of the ongoing war in Vietnam and the unfolding Watergate crisis, are ads that showcase Dacron polyester suits with lapels that are so wide that they resemble the outstretched wings of a supersonic Concorde jet. There are cringe-worthy patterned knit shirts and there are 7-inch brown side-zippered boots selling for $12.97 a pair, advertised as "high grade looks for your casual capers."

You could also rent a three-room apartment in New York's Greenwich Village for less than $300 a month, but I digress.

The look of America's pastime mirrored the look of America, for better or worse.

The aforementioned Pirates uniforms of 1970 were made of a blend of cotton and nylon, a bridge between the traditional flannel uniforms of yore and the double knits that contributed so much to the look of this golden age.

Double knit uniforms had several advantages over scratchy, old-fashioned flannels. For one thing, the new synthetic uniforms were lighter in weight. They were also easier to clean and, for our purposes, they allowed for the use of bold vibrant colors that represented a stark break from anything that had come before.

Chunky multi-striped sleeve trim also served as a hallmark of the time, adding brassy blocks of color to an area of the uniform that was previously sedate and relatively unembellished. This look was also extended to the neckline by many clubs.

Most MLB teams made the switch to knit uniforms in 1972 and, by the following season, the flannel era was completely dead and buried, with the Montreal Expos, Kansas City Royals, and New York Yankees representing the final converts to double knits.

Similar to the prevailing fashion of the day, these new uniforms were tight, form-fitting affairs. Willie Mays is credited with having jump-started the trend toward a more tapered, form-fitting uniform in the early sixties. By 1967, an informal poll revealed that half of the "tightest pants" in the major leagues belonged to San Francisco Giants players, including Mays.

While the closer fit might have looked great on some players, the new uniforms did not represent a flattering look for others. In 1971, the *Philadelphia Daily News* noted, "fat managers look especially silly in them." Just take a look at images of that classic baseball lifer, Don Zimmer, for example. Zimmer's big-league managerial career began in 1972, the same year that the San Diego Padres first wore their all-yellow/gold uniforms. He was forty-one years old at the time, not too far removed from the waning days of his nearly two decades as a professional ballplayer. He moved on to serve as skipper of the Boston Red Sox four years later, where Bill Lee famously referred to him as a "gerbil." A glance at the 1977 Red Sox yearbook reveals a photo of Zimmer in the Fenway dugout, deeply bathed in the shadows of a late summer New England afternoon, his belly stretched tight against his pullover jersey, undeniably overhanging his beltless pants.

The yellow/gold Padres' uniforms were perfectly contoured to the powerful physique of instant superstar Dave Winfield. The same sentiment applies to the Red Sox' uniform of the era as sported by an Adonis-like Jim Rice. But Zimmer, like many of his managerial brethren, was simply not well-suited for the tailoring of the time.

Starting in 1971, button-free knit uniforms popped up across the big leagues like so many spring tulips. The St. Louis Cardinals jumped on the bandwagon that season with new jerseys that permitted their time-honored "birds-on-bat" insignia to be displayed in one piece, unfettered by pointless, antiquated buttons.

* * *

The next season was accompanied by an avalanche of sartorial change, with a slew of clubs opting for a more contemporary look. Some teams seemingly dipped a toe into the water. Cleveland, for example, busted out new pullovers that showcased a decidedly sedate wordmark that read "Indians" in plain blocky red serif letterforms. The Atlanta Braves, on the other hand, dove right in to the deep end with a stunningly modern set of uniforms that truly broke new ground.

They were created by Wayland Moore, then the Braves' graphics director. Moore's uniforms utilized each component as distinct, separate units. For instance, the body of the jerseys stand in stark contrast to the sleeves, which feature a stylized, almost op-art representation of a feather. Moore focused on the totality of the uniform, taking into consideration the new lines and vast expanses that the lack of buttons and lines provided.

He viewed color as a critical component of his creations, shifting the club away from a dark navy blue to a more electric, royal blue; a tacit acknowledgement of the role of broadcast television, especially color TV.

"TV was coming into its own then, and the colors had to fit people's eyes, raw colors. When I looked at the Braves uniforms, I saw red, white, and blue. The old uniforms had no big blocks of color. My first sketches were very narrow in scope, and, as I progressed, the shapes got bigger and bigger."

Moore said that his original concepts called for a greater emphasis on red, which was squelched by Hank Aaron himself, a man who looked good in every uniform he ever wore throughout his epic career.

Aaron, along with Braves coach and fellow Hall of Famer Eddie Mathews, reviewed several sets of prototypes, including a red road jersey, putting them on and taking them in while walking around on the field at Atlanta Stadium. Moore says that Aaron chimed in with, "'Waylon—too much red. I like blue. Not red.' After that, we switched it to blue."

Thus spoke The Hammer, and the Braves' road uniform would be blue.

The look was accompanied by paneled caps of blue and white with a distinctive lowercase "a," another touch intended to nudge the club toward a more contemporary appearance.

Moore's original creations included stylized customized uniform numbers, too. "We wanted a number that was a little fancy," Moore told me. "Most sports numbers were not fancy." They were changed to a more conventional athletic block after a couple of seasons, but the overall optics remained in place when Aaron shattered Babe Ruth's career home run record on April 8, 1974, clad in Moore's home whites with blue, feathered sleeves. The jersey he wore that night is now displayed in Cooperstown, a silent witness to one of baseball's most significant historic achievements. The Braves' "mod" look remained intact for only four seasons, but Aaron's big moment helped catapult them into our eternal consciousness as arguably the most visible ambassador of the golden era of the ugly baseball uniform.

The Braves' look was comparatively refined when stacked up against some of its direct contemporaries. Don Zimmer's unfortunate 1972 Padres uniforms represent the first volley in a nearly constant bombardment of stylistic changes that the franchise has come to be known for among uniform geeks.

The '72 Padres' all yellow/gold garb was an odd one, pairing buttoned jerseys and beltless pants, trimmed in brown. And it was *all* yellow/gold and brown, with not even an outline of white or any other color to be found, although the club did wear white sanitary socks on the road the following season.

Dodgers' infielder Billy Grabarkewitz quipped to the *Los Angeles Times*, "they seem to glow in the dark. That will make it very difficult to pull the delayed steal."

Bob Bavasi, son of the Padres' first club president Buzzie Bavasi, provided some insight on the origins of that all-gold look—as well as the Padres' signature brown and gold paneled hats.

Bob assisted his father during his high school years as a self-described gofer, running ticker tape scores up to the radio booth and to the scoreboard operator while doing odd jobs around the ballpark. "In those days," he remembers, "expansion clubs were not very good and were not drawing very well, either."

> I recall being a high school senior in the fall of 1971, attending the general managers' meetings with my mom and dad and my younger brother, Bill (future GM of the California Angels and Seattle Mariners). There was a trade show there with uniform and cap suppliers—I remember walking through this rather small trade show with my mom; we saw the New Era cap booth, and they had a paneled hat on display there. It was black, with a white triangular panel. We asked if they could make up a sample in Padres colors, brown with a yellow gold triangle.
>
> That was that. The sample showed up and I recall suggesting to my dad "as long as we're doing this, then maybe the uniforms should change too."

Laughing, Bavasi says, "Buzzy was probably thinking 'maybe we can use them for both home and road,'" a nod to the fact that the Padres were trying to save money wherever possible in those days.

The thinking behind the uniforms was all about brand extension and getting the attention of potential fans for the young franchise. The Padres' 1972–73 all-gold uniforms sit high atop anyone's list of most flamboyant looks of the era, and a high school senior helped propel them forward.

It's safe to say that the golden era of the ugly baseball uniform peaked early. The kaleidoscope of vibrant colors that came to represent the era rolled onward, but some of the more revolutionary details that served as the foundation for the whole thing began to wick away by the end of the seventies.

The Boston Red Sox, fresh off their epic collapse of the previous season, introduced a new uniform set for 1979, and it represented the first retrenchment from the sartorial revolution that had character-ized the decade.[1]

* * *

Boston was one of the old school clubs that painted around the edges of their tried and true visual iden-tity. Their transition to modern times respected the past, but embraced the present with vigor and en-thusiasm. In 1974, the club went so far as to experiment with paneled caps; red in the front, surrounded by navy, before going with vibrant red headwear with a contrasting navy visor the following year.

Many Red Sox fans of a certain age remember this look with warmth and happiness. This is the look of the 1975 pennant winners: a fun, young team with rookies Jim Rice and Fred Lynn tearing up the American League all summer. It's the look that Carlton Fisk wore when he coaxed a fly ball to stay fair in the 12th inning of Game Six of the World Series against the Big Red Machine.

It's also the look that Mike Torrez wore when he gave up a different fly ball that just cleared Fenway Park's Green Monster, off the bat of Bucky Bleeping Dent in '78. And while no one can say with cer-tainty, that painful moment may well have been the thing that pushed the usually stodgy Red Sox back to the boringly refined old days when it came to their on-field identity.

The Sox abandoned their pullovers and beltless pants in favor of their fusty old look of yore—a but-toned jersey with red soutache trim at home, and flat, gray, unembellished road jerseys with a yawn-in-ducing navy blue "BOSTON" awkwardly spaced across the front. The road jerseys were utterly devoid

---

1 The 1978 Red Sox are remembered for one of the most epic collapses in baseball history. Boston went from being 14 games ahead of their hated rivals, the New York Yankees, to losing the AL East title in a one-game playoff tiebreaker. New York came into Fenway Park in early September and smoked the Red Sox, sweeping a four-game series while outscoring the home team, 42–9, in what was immediately dubbed "The Boston Mas-sacre." I was a fourteen-year-old Red Sox fan at the time, and I attended the final two games of the series—my first visit to Fenway. Little more than a month later, Bucky Dent would seal the deal with his pop-fly home run that finished off the Red Sox, forever dispatching them to baseball infamy.

of any sense of personality; they even eschewed the Sox' signature player number style in favor of a soulless, plain block font, also rendered in navy blue with no trim.

Belts were back, as were the navy blue road caps that dated back to the time of Jimmie Foxx and Lefty Grove.

*   *   *

Ronald Reagan's election as President of the United States in 1980 ushered in an era of conservatism that baseball seemed to take to heart.

The Kansas City Royals went back to buttons and belts in 1983. The San Diego Padres, a team with a propensity for defying notions of visual convention, did likewise the following year.

In 1983, the San Francisco Giants, fresh off a half-decade bender in black and orange pullovers, hired Bay Area design firm Sidjakov, Berman & Gomez to refresh their logo and uniforms. They went for what was described as a "contemporary interpretation of a traditional look," characterized by refined use of typography, minimal trim, and an overall clean presentation fronted, of course, by buttoned jerseys and belted pants.

A few years later Jerry Berman, a principal at SB&G, told Steve Hubbard of the *Pittsburgh Press* that the Giants' uniforms were the ones that changed everything. "The concept was to go back to tradition and get rid of the garish colors that happened during the early seventies, when they started looking like softball uniforms."

"Baseball uniforms *should* look traditional," he said, "because of the tradition of the sport itself." What a killjoy.

Sidjakov, Berman & Gomez created a new look for the Padres two years after their Giants makeover, and the results were uncannily similar—especially the road versions. While the Giants' traveling suits featured an interlocking "SF" on the left chests of their road jerseys, the Padres wore an interlocking "SD," identically placed and proportioned, in brown, as opposed to black, also with an orange outline.

After several years of chipping away, 1987 was the year the major-league uniforms took a determined step backward.

That season, eight of the twenty-six big-league clubs changed uniform designs. In a return to a more traditional aesthetic, elastic waistbands and pullover jerseys were out. Buttons and belts were back with a vengeance. An Associated Press story noted, "everything old is new when it comes to duds on the diamonds."

* * *

While trends come and go, the reason for this wholesale shift may well have been influenced by the fact that Rawlings, the venerable St. Louis–based sporting goods company, had just become MLB's official uniform supplier. Rawlings' five-year deal gave it the right to outfit big-league teams, as well as to sell replica jerseys at retail.

The timing of this was no accident. Commissioner Peter V. Ueberroth, fresh off his successful stint as chief of the profitable 1984 Los Angeles Olympic Summer Games, aggressively pursued a modernization of MLB's antiquated licensing and merchandising strategy, and the Rawlings deal was one very visible piece of his larger game plan.

The Rawlings logo was stitched near the bottom of the right sleeve of most teams' uniforms, the first time in MLB history that a manufacturer's name appeared on a conspicuous part of the uniform.

Rawlings' exclusive status afforded them an unprecedented influence on the look of the sport. It's also possible that they desired a streamlined template for use across all of the twenty-six big-league clubs for ease of manufacturing and selling to the public.

In 1987, the White Sox broke free from their tryst with modernity and experimentation, opting for unembellished, traditional uniforms. The Atlanta Braves settled in with a look that was pretty much a dead ringer for the outfits they wore in Milwaukee, back in the 1950s. The Astros—THE ASTROS—stripped back their signature rainbow look, and the Seattle Mariners, a pullover club from the time they began play a decade earlier, went with a set of flat, uninspired uniforms, utterly devoid of character.

The Pittsburgh Pirates eliminated their bicentennial-era pillbox hats. The Minnesota Twins cast aside their pullovers in favor of buttons, belts, and pinstripes and, in perhaps the harshest blow of all, the Oakland A's, now formally known again as "Athletics," reverted back to the boring old days, a thorough and complete repudiation of the sartorial revolution that Charlie Finley sparked a quarter century earlier.

The Athletics' jerseys were now traditionally tailored, with script letterforms and TV numbers that were highly reminiscent of their fellow Californians, the Los Angeles Dodgers. Green and gold remained, but the effect was far more sedated. Gray road uniforms helped round out the ultimate capitulation to the forces of conservatism.

The golden era of the ugly baseball uniform was now dead. If it had a tombstone it would no doubt be a gaudy one, a conspicuous and loud outlier among all of the dignified and somber white and gray markers that might surround it, and there's no question in my mind that fans of the ugly uniform would come from far and wide to mourn, bearing artificial flowers.

The Atlanta Braves' 1972 visual reboot represented a bold, colorful departure from their previously sedate appearance.

Uniform collector Bill Henderson notes that the uniforms were cheaply constructed. "They began to shrink rapidly with the first washing, until after a few washings they had become unwearable," he says. "The club then decided to have the uniforms dry-cleaned after each game. Surviving examples are shrunken and puckered and many are stained, reportedly the result of a fire in the dry cleaning plant where they were being stored."

San Diego coasted into the doubleknit era with an all-gold ensemble that blurred the lines between home *and* road sets and blinded National League opponents. The uniforms were worn in 1972 and 1973, after which the team nearly moved to Washington, DC, although that had nothing to do with these loud uniforms.

The San Diego Padres wore this jersey at home in 1979. It features huge, bold blocks of color and a lowercase "padres" wordmark that Ron Burgundy would surely have found both stylish and attractive. The look lasted but a single season, a one year wonder and a "bridge uniform" to a brighter future. The club spruced things up the following year when they injected orange into the brown and gold mix, thus inspiring Steve Garvey's famous "taco" comparison. That jersey accompanied the Padres to their 1984 World Series appearance, the first in in club history.

The San Diego Padres of the 1970s and early '80s changed uniform designs nearly as often as George M. Steinbrenner changed Yankee managers. In 1980 the Padres trotted out these uniforms, which they would stick with for a whole five seasons.

The jerseys, buttressed by the addition of the color orange to their usual brown and yellow/gold palette, must have agreed with the club. They won their first National League pennant dressed up in these duds in 1984, after which they cast them aside, once again proving themselves to be the era's most indecisively attired franchise.

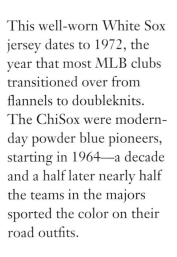

This well-worn White Sox jersey dates to 1972, the year that most MLB clubs transitioned over from flannels to doubleknits. The ChiSox were modern-day powder blue pioneers, starting in 1964—a decade and a half later nearly half the teams in the majors sported the color on their road outfits.

The Chicago Cubs, a club with steadily staid visual habits, transitioned to new pullover doubleknit uniforms in 1972.

While the home sets looked pretty much like the flannel togs they replaced, the road jerseys were very decidedly un-Cubbish. Snazzy red, white, and blue striping was in, along with very weird-looking centered numbers on the fronts, an effect that smacked of something that the NFL's Chicago Bears might wear.

These jerseys lasted but a year, but the experiment was rewarded late in the season when Fergie Jenkins hit Joe Pepitone right between the numbers for a game-winning 46-yard touchdown pass.

1973 OAKLAND A's   WORLD CHAMPIONS

FIRST ROW (left to right)—Reggie Jackson, Catfish Hunter, Pat Bourque, Batboy Ron Pieraldi, Dick Green, Vic Davalillo and Bill North.

SECOND ROW (left to right)—Bert Campaneris, Vida Blue, Paul Lindblad, Coach Jerry Adair, Coach Vern Hoscheit, Manager Dick Williams, Coach Irv Noren, Coach Wes Stock, Sal Bando and Gene Tenace.

THIRD ROW (left to right)—Trainer Joe Romo, traveling secretary Jim Bank, An Mangual, Jesus Alou, Joe Rudi, John Odom, Mike Andrews, Ted Kubiak, and equ ment manager Frank Ciensczyk.

FOURTH ROW (left to right)—Horacio Pina, Ken Holtzman, Deron Johnson, Ro Fingers, Billy Conigliaro, Ray Fosse, Darold Knowles and Allan Lewis.

(Photograph courtesy of the National Baseball Hall of Fame Museum, Cooperstown, NY)

INNING

5

THE EXPOS,
RACING STRIPES, AND
THE LOOK OF THE '80s

The Expos, Racing Stripes, and the Look of the '80s

There are two kinds of people in this world. There are those who think that the Montreal Expos' logo and uniforms were strange and ugly, and then there are the rest of us. I'd be remiss if I didn't discuss the singularly weird—but undeniably charming—optics of *Nos Amours*, the first MLB team based outside of the United States of America.

The Expos were born in 1969, an expansion franchise with a totally blank slate, playing in a progressive city that was clearly on the move. Montreal had recently hosted the wildly successful Expo 67, a World's Fair attended by more than fifty million people, a landmark exposition and a source of civic pride for which the ballclub was named.

This freshly minted team had license to do something different with their visual identity, and they came through in spades. Their red, white, and blue logo was introduced to the public on January 14, 1969. Just exactly what the hell it is has been continually debated ever since.

The logo, created by Canadian design firm Stewart & Morrison, was the subject of bewilderment and snark right from the start. *Montreal Gazette* columnist Ted Blackman covered the press conference at which the symbol was unveiled and he wrote about it the very next day. He said that John McHale, the club president, "unveil(ed) the logo to the same thundering silence that greeted the announcement of the name 'Expos' . . . the club president feels it is distinctive and projects the image of all of Canada. Never could figure out those ink blots, either."

The official explanation from that day reads as follows: "A mod-like 'm' encompassing an 'e,' italicized for forward movement." The colors, it was noted, were identical to those used by hockey's Montreal Canadiens, *rouge, blanc, et bleu*.

Let's stop right here take a deeper look at this logo. OK, I see the "m." And there's definitely an "e" in there. But isn't that a "b," at the far right side? And, if that's the case, does that stand for "Montreal baseball," or, perhaps "*merci beaucoup?*"

Wait, it sure looks like there's a lowercase "l" squeezed into the middle of the whole thing. "Expos League Baseball." "*Expos le baseball.*"

All these years after the Expos left for Washington, DC, there are still conspiracy theories about the logo. It contains a "cb" for team owner Charles Bronfman. Or maybe the whole thing is "eb" for Ellen Bronfman, Charles' daughter. The truth may never be fully known, but one thing is for certain: the Expos logo unquestionably represents the Grassy Knoll of all baseball logos.

The uniforms were unleashed a little more than a week after the logos were introduced, and were modeled by club controller Harry Renaud. The look was, in retrospect, a dignified one, even if it did break away from convention in small dollops. The team's funky logo was placed on the left chest of both home and road jerseys, flanked by customized player numbers that are both refined and understated. The sleeve trim was quite restrained as well, and the whole look gave off a whiff of modernity, without at all reeking of anything garish.

What really got people's attention were the caps: those red, white, and blue paneled oddities that broke new ground and reminded more than a few folks of beanies. Commenting on the chapeaus, Montreal manager Gene Mauch said "all it needs is a little propeller on top."

A UPI story from the beginning of April noted that Expos' caps "will be the first thing anyone notices," and called them out as "gaudy affairs." One *Pittsburgh Press* columnist wrote, "they look like something [celebrity gossip columnist] Hedda Hopper might wrap her garbage in."

Early in the season, Milton Richman, later inducted in the "writer's wing" of the Baseball Hall of Fame, penned an article which focused on the unusual headwear. "There was this thing about their hats and how ridiculous they looked," he wrote. Richman quoted pitcher Jim "Mudcat" Grant, who defended the caps in the face of ridicule and adversity. Grant noted that other teams in Spring Training made fun of the Expos' hats, but that he liked them. "The other teams kept looking at our caps and laughing . . . every time we'd go somewhere to play an exhibition game the other team would look at us and say 'here come the fellas with the funny caps.'"

While the Expos' paneled caps may have looked funny to outsiders, the locals snapped them up. The *Washington Post* reported that the team "reaped almost as much from the sale of . . . caps as [fellow NL expansion club] San Diego reaped from gate receipts," with more than three hundred thousand lids sold that first year alone.

Montreal's logo was a cradle-to-grave affair, used from their very first game in 1969 right up until the final one in 2004. Sadly, the signature hats were cast aside in 1992, in favor of an all-blue model that never seemed to highlight the "elb" nearly as well as when it was placed against a stark white background.

For all the Expos' visual nonconformity, there remains this fact: the Montreal Expos played a total of 5,698 games across their 36 seasons, and never once did they wear anything other than button down jerseys and traditional belted pants.

The Expos, along with a few other franchises, adopted a "racing stripe" look in the early 1980s. In Montreal's case these were 2 inches wide: half red, half blue, which ran from the neckline of the jersey all the way down the sides, extending onto the pants.

Although this was a design feature that had been used previously, the combination of bold vertical striping and form-fitting uniforms cut a truly modern and dynamic appearance, especially in an era when stealing bases was all the rage. Montreal outfielder Ron LeFlore swiped 97 bases in 1980, the first year his team wore the racing stripes, and he looked like a streamlined, fast-moving vehicle while doing so.

The Philadelphia Phillies pioneered the stripy thing in 1970, but it took a while for other clubs to glom on. Oddly, the Dodgers (of all teams), still outfitted in old-fashioned flannels, added bold blue stripes to their road uniforms in 1971, but they soon came to their senses and abandoned the experiment after that one single season.

The Mariners and Indians both sported the racing stripes, and the 1986 New York Mets won the World Series while wearing them. When Jesse Orosco struck out Boston's Marty Barrett to end that Series, he dropped to his knees and tossed his glove high up into the air, the bold stripes of his uniform pointed skyward toward the heavens. This was clearly a tribute to the divine forces that had conspired in the Mets' favor throughout that historic October.

The Astros' signature rainbow stripes, banished to their jersey sleeves after having been pried from the guts of the jerseys, would have really been something to see had they extended down the sides of their pants, but the club opted for a single wide navy stripe instead.

The last MLB club to regularly wear the racing stripe look was a weird one—as a matter of fact, I'll bet that you don't even remember it.

The Detroit Tigers, usually a role model for sartorial restraint and consistency, went all-in with five-banded racing stripes on their 1994 road uniforms, worn but 57 times in that strike-shortened year that cost MLB its entire postseason.

That marked the surprisingly belated end of the line for a look that, in retrospect, was to 1980s baseball what Sheena Easton was to 1980s pop music: a ubiquitous and somewhat exotic presence that now seems dated and kind of silly.

The MYSTERIES of the EXPOS LOGO

OVERALL SHAPE IS AN "M"

[see?]

IS THIS AN "L"?

"eb?"

EXPOS le BASEBALL?

MOD LIKE

"E" for "Expos"

ITALICIZED FOR FORWARD MOVEMENT

"b" STANDS FOR "baseball"

A FIELD GUIDE TO RACING STRIPES OF THE 80s & 90s

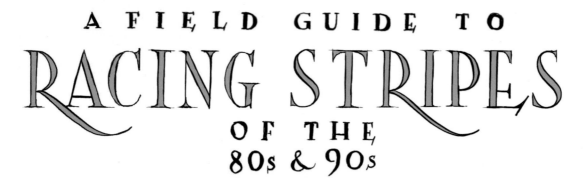

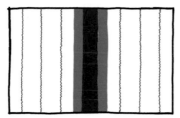

NEW YORK METS

MONTREAL EXPOS

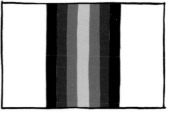

HOUSTON ASTROS

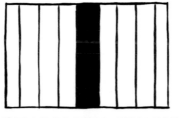

PHILADELPHIA PHILLIES

CLEVELAND INDIANS

SEATTLE MARINERS

DETROIT TIGERS

The 1986 National League Championship Series pitted the Houston Astros, resplendent in their road uniform racing stripes, against the New York Mets, who were outfitted in racing stripes both home *and* away. The Mets won an epic 16-inning Game Six to take the series, a contest which also marked the final appearance of the Astros' classic rainbow jerseys.

THE EXPOS, RACING STRIPES, AND THE LOOK OF THE '80S   83

The Expos and their powder blue road uniforms represent a serendipitous pairing, a harmonious synthesis of color and graphic elements that just seems perfectly suited for the stylish city of Montreal and its ballclub. Many teams wore the powder blues, but the Expos' racing striped powder blues, worn from 1980–91, reign supreme— perfectly balanced, vibrant, uniquely recognizable.

Many years removed from its last active usage, Montreal's logo—a "mod-like 'm' encompassing an 'e,' italicized for forward movement"—is still the subject of conjecture and debate. It is a symbol shrouded in mystery, a foreign logo for a foreign team, rouge, blanc, blue, et incroyable.

There is so much to really, really hate about this jersey (sorry, Astros fans). After the Roman Empire fell to the hands of the Visigoths in the fifth century, many surviving architectural remnants of its greatness were repurposed, often as barely recognizable pieces of a distant golden age. Such was the case with the Astros' signature tequila sunrise uniforms, bits and pieces of which are seen here, several seasons after their decline and fall.

The rainbow guts have been greatly diminished and exiled to the jersey sleeves. The modern letterforms survive here, mostly intact, but are now oddly spaced and interrupted by archaic buttons. The jersey is off-white, a cream color that just seems wrong.

There is beauty buried far below the surface here, but you have to look really hard to find it.

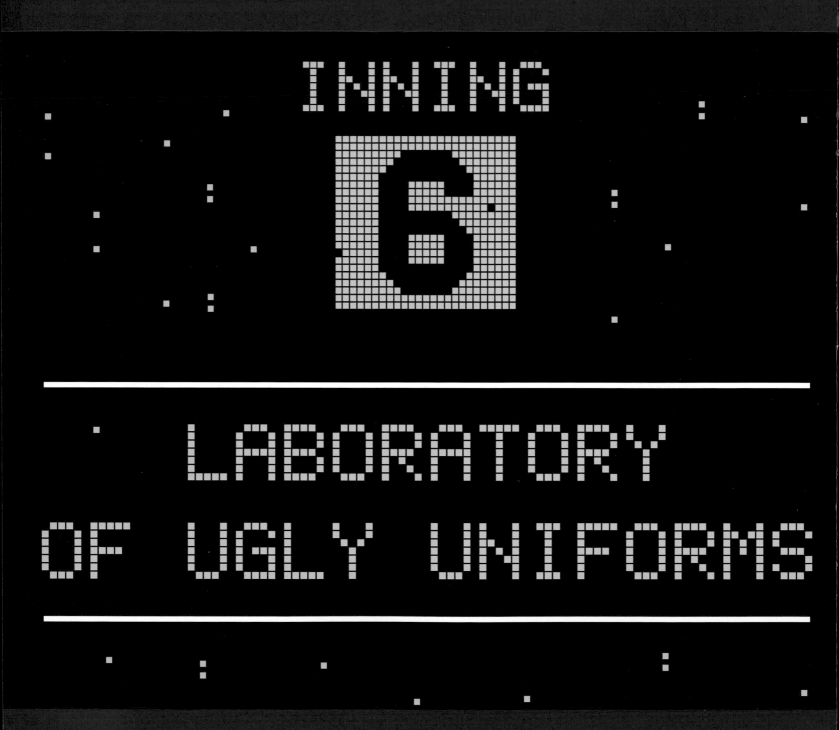

INNING 6

LABORATORY OF UGLY UNIFORMS

Laboratory of Ugly Uniforms

Welcome, my friends, to the laboratory of ugly uniforms! A place where experimentation is always encouraged and innovation is our constant companion.

Over there on the left are the uniforms of the 2016 Arizona Diamondbacks, resplendently decorated in gradated patterns from head to toe. No detail has been overlooked here, as witnessed by the bottoms of the team's pants. Contrary to what you are thinking, no, the entire team did *not* stride through the aftermath of a zombie apocalypse before arriving here at the lab.

I'd urge you all to take particular note of their dark gray road uniforms, a gray so dark that they conjure up thoughts of Spinal Tap lead guitarist Nigel Tufnel. "There's something about this that's so gray, it's like how much more gray could this be? And the answer is none. None more gray."

Let's move along now, shall we?

Here, on your left, are the 2004–11 Toronto Blue Jays. Pardon me, the JAYS, as all references to the word "blue" have been omitted. The actual color blue, while not altogether eliminated, has been benched in favor of black and silver, along with "graphite," a color that was thought to have been the next big thing back in the early 2000s.

On your right are the black uniforms worn by the Kansas City Royals—I'll bet you don't even remember these, right? And here, safely enclosed in a climate-controlled glass case, are the dark blue, pinstriped road uniforms of the 1925 Chicago White Sox, a look that appropriately evokes that of a prohibition-era Windy City bootlegger.

The uniforms of the expansion Tampa Bay Devil Rays, ladies and gentleman, merit our attention here. As you can see, their jersey lettering incorporated a unique gradated effect, a bold experiment that was right at home in the late 1990s. Let's recall the fact that this was a time when designers were pushing the boundaries of digital design technology, their late nights spent behind huge CRT monitors, cold bottles of Zima at the ready, their work speedily delivered to distant clients via dial-up modems.

Over here are our satin jerseys, designed to shimmer and shine under bright stadium lights, worn back when night games were new. Behold these sleeveless numbers, an innovation that Cincinnati Reds slugger Ted Kluszewski looked great in both at night AND during the day—sun's out, guns out, after all. Let me interrupt our tour with a relevant piece of trivia. Three men have ended the World Series with a walk-off hit while wearing a vest. Can you name them?

Well, they are Bill Mazeroski of the Pirates in 1960, Edgar Renteria of the Marlins in 1997, and Luis Gonzalez of the Diamondbacks in 2001. How about that!

There are, of course, many experiments that were once ridiculed, but still stuck. Uniform numbers, for instance, were roundly criticized when the 1916 Cleveland Indians first introduced them to the big leagues. Players felt that it was not a look becoming of a professional athlete, and sportswriters made fun of them.

Legendary baseball innovator Bill Veeck added names to his White Sox' jerseys in 1960, and opposing players snickered. Batting helmets, pullover jerseys, and colorful graphics all were questioned at one time, only to be eventually recognized as common parts of the visual culture of baseball.

Okay, folks, come along, let's continue the tour. I want to draw your attention to these white baseball caps, worn by the New York Mets for a handful of games in 1997. Note their resemblance to those worn by ice cream vendors . . .

The Seattle Pilots represented the Pacific Northwest in the American League for one single season, 1969, before packing up the moving vans and shifting to Milwaukee to be reborn as the Brewers. Aside from serving as the backdrop for Jim Bouton's classic *Ball Four*, the Pilots are remembered for their singularly weird uniforms, which included caps with "scrambled eggs." The jerseys were chock full of odd details but the weirdest ones were left on the cutting room floor—the pants were originally supposed to have featured blue belt loops and a gold belt buckle.

Pictured here is former Mets phenom Dwight Gooden, looking entirely out of place in the uniform of the 2000 Tampa Bay Devil Rays. The Rays' inaugural gradated look lasted only three seasons before giving way to something far more conventional and traditional.

The Toronto Blue Jays were transformed into the black-clad "Jays" for eight seasons, starting in 2004. An update of their progressive original look replaced this trend-driven off-brand experiment, a pivot backwards that was widely applauded.

When the Kansas City Royals joined the American League in 1969 they looked, more or less, like an alternate reality version of the Dodgers, which is not such a bad thing when you think about it. Royal blue and white, accented with a touch of gold, have been KC hallmarks across the breadth of their entire history.

In the early 2000s, however, things started to go off the rails. The Royals jumped onto the "let's add black" bandwagon that was embraced by several clubs at the time, and the ultimate result was this little-remembered alternate road jersey that was worn only in 2006.

Kansas City lost 100 games that season. The club reverted back to their core look, one that accompanied them to a World Series championship in 2015.

Uniform history was made at Shea Stadium on April 15, 1997. That night, Major League Baseball honored the legacy of Jackie Robinson by retiring his number 42. The host New York Mets showed up for the occasion dressed as ice cream men.

History aside, that evening marked the debut of the Mets' white caps, worn just a handful of times that season before being traded to a Carvel stand in West Hempstead for a vanilla soft serve cone and a Cookie Puss cake to be named later.

In 1998, the New York Mets supplemented their traditional blue and orange color scheme with black, a look that accompanied them to the World Series a couple of years later. The club even applied black to an alternate version of their classic "skyline" logo. Black remained an official part of the Mets' designated color palette through the 2013 season.

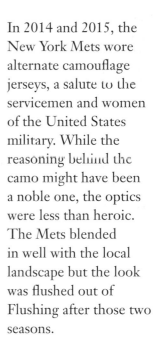

In 2014 and 2015, the New York Mets wore alternate camouflage jerseys, a salute to the servicemen and women of the United States military. While the reasoning behind the camo might have been a noble one, the optics were less than heroic. The Mets blended in well with the local landscape but the look was flushed out of Flushing after those two seasons.

Arizona's 2016 uniform reboot included very dark gray road uniforms, a polarizing feature that some observers found refreshingly unique and others found to be reminiscent of the aftermath of a charred campfire.

A young franchise with less than two decades of history can take chances in a way that the Yankees and Cardinals of the world cannot. The Diamondbacks' rethinking of the standard gray road uniform provided them a trademark appearance and garnered them a great deal of attention, for better or for worse.

Remember that time in middle school when you inadvertently stepped on a packet of ketchup in the cafeteria and everyone made fun of you for the rest of the day? Well, the 2016 Arizona Diamondbacks' pants conjured up distant memories of that very same condiment catastrophe.

The D'Backs 2016 uniform refresh held nothing back, and part of that radical redesign was the inclusion of a red gradated pattern at the southern end of their pants that also closely resembled the aftermath of a stroll through a zombie apocalypse.

This particular design feature was roundly questioned by fans and players alike and was abandoned after but a single season.

August 25–27, 2017, represents a watershed event in the long history of ugly baseball uniforms. This was the moment that "Miller Time," "Pickles," and "Beef" took the field of play for MLB Players Weekend, expressing their individuality in flamboyant uniforms that left some fans grumbling and others wanting for more.

When Good Teams Go Bad

A few classic, well-regarded team looks have taken meandering detours along the way, only to circle back to where they probably always belonged.

The St. Louis Cardinals are hailed by most observers for having one of the best looks in the sport, even by some Cubs fans. Their "birds on bat" have evolved over the decades but, nearly a century after their debut, for many, they represent the gold standard of what a baseball uniform can (and should) look like.

The seeds of the Cardinals' now familiar uniform originated at a dinner held by the Men's Fellowship Club of the Ferguson, Missouri, Presbyterian Church on February 16, 1921. Cardinals' vice president and general manager Branch Rickey spoke at that event and was taken by the table decorations, which were created by congregant Allie May Schmidt. Her creation—cardboard cutouts of red cardinal birds, perched atop twigs made out of string—inspired Rickey.

Rickey then commissioned Allie May's father, Edward H. Schmidt—head of the art department at the Woodward and Tiernan Printing Co.—to create artwork for the Cardinals' uniforms, which made their debut in April 1922.

The *St. Louis Post-Dispatch* readied the public for what they were about to see:

"Fans who gather at Sportsman's Park for the spring series game tomorrow will receive an eye shock when the new Cardinals uniforms dawn on them. Across the shirt front they will see an emblem that strongly resembles a sample of Aztec picture writing. The Cardinals' new crest consists of a black war club, oblique, surmounted by two cardinal birds, rampant.

"It will be by far the gaudiest bit of baseball heraldry that ever dazzled a fan's eyes. The emblem will be worn on both home and abroad uniforms."

Despite a couple of brief interruptions in the late twenties, the birds served as the backdrop for a string of outstanding St. Louis teams, with multiple World Series titles to brag about. In 1956, however, all of this came to a grinding halt.

That season, general manager Frank Lane scrapped the birds in favor of a simpler approach, an unembellished set of home and road jerseys with the word "Cardinals" stretched across the jerseys in script. The famous birds had flown the coop.

When asked about the change, Lane told the *Detroit Free Press*, "(w)hy'd we change it? That's simple. How can you impress any team with your hitting when you got a couple of birds perched on either end of your bat?" He also cited the fact that the team had finished in seventh place the previous year.

The move was not embraced by fans. The 1956 squad won a few more games than the 1955 version and moved on up to fourth place, but the birds were reinstated the following season, and there they have stayed ever since.

"You can say I've had to eat crow for doing away with the birds," Lane told the *Sporting News*. "I can see why everybody wanted to give me the bird."

Like many teams of the seventies, the Cardinals made the move to pullovers and beltless pants. They also opted for powder blue road uniforms for a while, but they still *looked* like the Cardinals.

In the court of public opinion, a classic team is allowed to paint around the edges of their masterpiece, but that's as far as they are allowed to go.

The Detroit Tigers, along with the Cardinals, comfortably fall into "classic" territory. The Tigers Old English "D" is one of baseball's most enduring icons, a venerable symbol of Detroit that actually dates back to the Tigers days in the Western League of the late 1890s.

In 1960, the Tigers went "off brand" for a single season, dropping the time-honored "D" that had been a Motor City staple on their home jerseys since 1934. Newly installed club president Bill DeWitt, determined to make significant changes across the entire franchise, made the decision, calling it an "experiment."

DeWitt made a lot of noise that year, but the Tigers finished in sixth place. Home attendance plummeted, fans were less than happy, and DeWitt left the club after just around a year in power.

As if to erase any visual evidence of the unhappy, short-lived marriage, the Tigers brought the "D" back in 1961, saying that the club was "restoring a broken tradition."

Since then, the Tigers have held tight to their home look through seasons both good and bad, but the team did have a one-day dalliance with an alternate jersey, back in 1995.

On May 7 of that year, the Tigers absorbed a 12–1 shellacking at the hands of the Boston Red Sox, but, more importantly for our purposes, they did so wearing dark blue alternate jerseys that depicted a snarling tiger, crawling through the familiar "D." While these jerseys were originally designed to have been worn with—wait for it—pinstriped pants, the team went with solid white bottoms that afternoon.

The getup was never worn again.

Teams without a winning tradition generally have license to change their look, as do newer franchises in markets with fan bases that have little in the way of heritage to genuflect toward.

The Arizona Diamondbacks, established in 1998, have license to trot out seven different regular game jerseys. The aforementioned Yankees, on the other hand, are expected to adhere to their enduring look. In fact, out-of-towners who attend a game at Yankee Stadium in the Bronx do so expecting to see the pinstripes, an affirming visage that provides must-see visual flavor to the whole experience.

When the New York Giants packed up and moved across the continent to San Francisco in 1958, they brought with them their very handsome uniforms, trimmed in orange and black. This core look was retained right up until 1977, when the club broke with tradition, introducing home pullovers with script letterforms and vivid orange road jerseys. The next year the Giants added black jerseys into the mix. In hindsight, this era seems like a weird departure for this particular franchise. The team pivoted back to something more conventional in 1983, finally returning to something that looked like their New York togs of yore, affirmation of the fact that, yes, you can go home again.

The Detroit Tigers discarded decades of Motor City visual equity in 1960 when they eliminated the Old English "D" from their home jerseys in favor of this cursive approach. The club brought the trademark "D" back one year later, saying that they were "restoring a broken tradition."

On May 7, 1995, the Detroit Tigers wore these navy blue alternate jerseys in a home game against the Boston Red Sox. The team absorbed a 12–1 loss and never wore them again.

As alternate jerseys go, this one is not bad, but it represents a strange departure from the Tigers' tried-and true uniform routine. While many clubs added alternates in the 1990s, the Tigers' brief flirtation with a navy jersey seems weird and off-brand, a fleeting foray into unfamiliar territory that they tried once, had a bad experience with, then swore off forever.

The San Francisco Giants were among the last stragglers to convert from old-fashioned flannel uniforms to doubleknits, finally making the transition in 1973. Four years later the club went nuts, at least by Giants standards. They adopted a totally new look, accompanied by wide sleeve striping, pullover jerseys, sansabelt pants, and screamingly conspicuous orange road jerseys. They even wore orange sanitary socks for a few years, an especially bold fashion statement for what had always been a tradition-bound organization.

The only memorable aspect of the 1956 St. Louis Cardinals was their uniforms, which dropped the team's trademark "birds on bat" after more than three decades of nearly continual usage. Redbird fans spoke up, and the team restored the traditional configuration the following season. While these 1956 uniforms are neither weird nor ugly, they do represent a strange detour from one of the game's most time-honored looks.

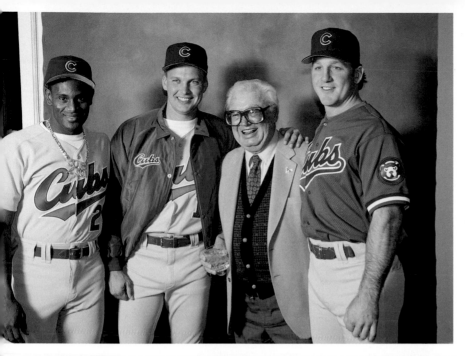

For three seasons (1994–96) the Chicago Cubs morphed into the Cuban national team while on the road. The Cubs sported these jerseys, which looked to many like they read "Cuba," especially when viewed from a distance.

Legendary Cubs announcer Harry Caray is seen here at center, celebrating the uniform unveiling with one in a series of fortifying Cuba Libres.

The Chicago Cubs have featured plenty of different looks since they began play in the nineteenth century, but few have been castigated more than the vest-style uniforms that they wore from 1940–42.
The jerseys were made of a knit material and designed for ease of movement. Immediately upon introduction, players hated them and the press happily piled on. Matters were made worse when the team opted for powder blue road jerseys in 1941, prompting the *Sporting News* to beg the question "(h)ave the Cubs developed a pantywaist inferiority complex?"

When the club went back to a more conventional appearance in 1943 one newspaper headline read "Cubs Abandon Freak Uniforms This Season."

The Los Angeles Dodgers are the very model of visual consistency—blindingly white uniforms at home, elegant gray on the road, bound together by the classic blue "Dodgers" script, kissed by red player numbers.

For a handful of games in the summer of 1999 the club deviated from their familiar look with blue jerseys, including this one, which was worn on June 5, 1999, at Dodger Stadium.

Dodger pitcher Chan Ho Park made that day even more memorable when he drop-kicked Anaheim hurler Tim Belcher, a costly martial arts demonstration that earned Park a seven-game suspension and a $3,000 fine.

Angels shortstop Gary DiSarcina told the *Los Angeles Times*, "The last time I saw someone kick somebody in a fight, it was my little sister kicking my brother for taking her Barbie doll."

While the game was an ugly one, the Dodgers' uniforms were not all that bad, even if they were decidedly un-Dodger-like with all of those outlines and all that silver trim, a brief and weird departure from their usual on-field garb.

In 2007, the Pittsburgh Pirates introduced a new alternate home uniform: a red sleeveless jersey that many observers likened to another Steel City stalwart, Heinz 57 ketchup.

Fans and players immediately savaged the uniforms. While red had been a little-noticed tertiary color in the Pirates' color palette for a decade when the uniforms made their debut, it was way too much for many observers.

The Buccos ditched the look after just two seasons, a sensible return to their more familiar core black and gold colors.

The always fashionable New York Yankees have dodged a few potential sartorial disasters over the course of their long and storied history.

In 1915, the club announced that they would be wearing new road uniforms that contained broad pinstripes of green, blue, and red. Yankees co-owner Tillinghast L'Hommedieu "Cap" Huston and manager Bill Donovan grappled over the design of the uniforms for months. Their indecision took on a greater sense of urgency when the club donated the previous season's togs to the Sing Sing prison baseball team. Evidence is murky on whether the multicolored striped uniforms ever saw the light of day.

Nearly six decades later the Yankees seriously considered a new road uniform that was essentially a reversal of the home version—navy blue with white pinstripes and a white interlocking "NY." Another near miss occurred in 1976. The *Sporting News* published an item in February of that year which stated that the club, "departing from longtime tradition," would be wearing gray uniforms with navy blue pinstripes on the road.

The Yankees' road uniforms have been gray—never navy blue—with no pinstripes, multicolored or otherwise, since 1918. It's an understated look that's undisputedly Yankee-like, a bit fusty but totally in sync with the visual DNA of the franchise.

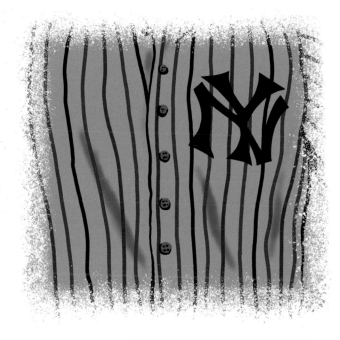

The Evening Star.

WASHINGTON, D. C., FRIDAY, MARCH 5, 1915

Manager Bill Donovan has picked out an entirely new layout of uniforms for his Yankees, and the New York scribes, after inspecting the new apparel, unite in saying he has batted .1000 in the fashion league. Take this slant at the design of the road uniform: "On a background of Confederate gray there are blue, cardinal and green stripes, with caps of the same material, with blue visors. The stockings are of dark blue with white cross bars. The blouses have military collars, and are form-fitting at the waist. The pants are of cavalry cut, reinforced; belts of new design. **The monogram on the blouses is in two colors.**"

Diamond Duds

Sometimes, in life, things don't fit into neat little buckets.

Here, then, are the stragglers, the outliers, the waifs. This is our very own Island of Misfit Uniforms, a hodgepodge of lousy livery, a curated assortment of abhorrent apparel.

Baseball's past is chock full of weird uniforms—memorable disasters, strange freaks, and sideshow-worthy anomalies. Sometimes these are the result of trends, which, being inherently trendy, come as quickly as they go. Think sleeveless jerseys, or vests, or the preponderance of pointless black uniforms that the 1990s and early 2000s gifted us.

Some of these uniforms are the result of bad decisions; others spring forth from attention-seeking promotions, and some emerged via plain old bad taste.

The 1956 Cincinnati Redlegs, for example, wore road jerseys that showcased a terrifying depiction of their Mr. Red mascot.[1] In 2012, the Tampa Bay Rays unveiled a fun and fanciful "fauxback" uniform that conjured up the optics of the disco era, which took place decades before the Rays franchise even existed.

More recently, for three games in August 2017, Major League Baseball loosened up its usual uniform restrictions in honor of their "Players Weekend" promotion.

That weekend, MLB unleashed a 72-hour barrage of brightly colored pullover jerseys with contrasting sleeves, accompanied by player nicknames on the backs. Some sobriquets were predicable, such as Ian Happ's "Happer" and Blake Wood's "Blake." Others, however, were memorably inventive. Dodgers'

---

1   Today's Cincinnati Reds club dates to 1890, when the franchise shifted from the American Association to the National League. The Reds name, of course, harkens back to Cincinnati's legendary Red Stockings of the late 1860s. In 1953, the club officially designated themselves as "Redlegs," a reaction to the "Red Scare" and to America's supercharged political climate of the day. That moment had passed by 1959, when the club reverted back to being called "Reds."

reliever Ross Stripling's jersey read "Chicken Strip." Seattle's Kyle Seager went with "Corey's Brother" for his nickname, as his younger brother, Corey, has taken the league by storm since being brought up by the Dodgers in 2015. San Diego's Brad Hand made MLB history by becoming the first man to sport the word "Brotato" on a big-league diamond.

For the first time in their storied, visually reserved history, the tradition-bound New York Yankees wore names on the backs of their jerseys. Which, incidentally, featured no buttons—also a franchise first.

Keith Olbermann has seen a lot of Yankee games over the last half century. When I asked him what his thoughts were on these decidedly un-Yankee-like togs, he did not disappoint.

"They looked like the unlicensed knockoff Yankee T-shirts you used to be able to buy in the cheap Army/Navy stores up near the Grand Concourse in the Bronx," he said. "Not the shops across from Yankee Stadium. The ones several blocks away. And not in the front of the store. In the back with the flip-flops and bucket hats. In 1980."

* * *

The Chicago White Sox hosted the first "Turn Back the Clock" promotion back in 1990. Since then, baseball fans have been able to see some of the sport's most memorable uniforms of yore, in action, worn by contemporary players: a fun celebration of the game's rich, visual history.

There is no denying the novel treat of seeing, for instance, the Houston Astros in their polyester rainbow look. The same applies to modern interpretations of the St Louis Cardinals' classic uniforms or some of the great togs worn by Negro League teams of the distant past. But there have been many other instances where the past would probably have been best left way behind.

Uniforms of the 1970s and early '80s were form-fitting affairs. Ballplayers of the early twenty-first century preferred a more "relaxed" fit. Put the two together and you get a strange hybrid, something akin to seeing Civil War reenactors communicating via cell phone.

Trying to make order out of chaos is a fool's errand. Let us embrace these misfits and celebrate them—the bold, the trendy, the weird and wonderful mistakes that simply cannot be ignored—for better or worse.

The Anaheim Angels wore these jerseys once and only once—on July 2, 1997, against their Freeway Series neighbors, the Los Angeles Dodgers.

History was made in the fourth inning when Anaheim leftfielder Tony Phillips became the first player in MLB history to instigate a benches-clearing brawl while wearing a jersey with periwinkle sleeves.

Periwinkle, deep sky blue, lighter sky blue, navy, red, bronze, and gold. These were the colors of the 1997–2001 Anaheim Angels, a Disney production that gave us uniforms with faux vests, a chunky outlined and shadowed winged "A" logo, and a whole lot of derisive snickers.

This look piled on the details in a big way, but it actually could have been worse. The originally approved uniforms called for double pinstripes, rendered in periwinkle and navy, along with widely flared banded stripes around the shoulders that looked like something out of a dystopian science fiction movie.

The *Los Angeles Times* polled readers on the uniforms when they were launched in February 1997, and sentiment was overwhelmingly negative. "One unidentified caller," they wrote, "actually accused the new apparel of looking 'like something my five-year-old kid would wear in a Little League game. That little wing on the 'A,' that's pretty cute. That's really going to intimidate Roger Clemens and Jimmy Key.'"

Vests were once a big deal in MLB, and some teams looked great in them. The Colorado Rockies, on the other hand, looked like the cast of a *Star Trek* spinoff.

San Diego is a navy town and a place with strong, deep military connections. The hometown Padres began wearing camouflage jerseys in 2000 with a warm-hued woodland pattern that has since evolved. The club has worn digital patterns used by the US Navy and Marines as well as a Navy SEAL desert version. The camo look is a popular one in San Diego, a relevant fit for their particular market.

Minnesota donned these fire engine red jerseys for a few games in 1997. They made their debut on April 6 of that season, and the Kansas City Royals hammered the Twins by a score of 12–2. ESPN announcers christened them the "Dairy Queen" jerseys in tribute to the Minnesota-based ice cream outfit's bright red logo, as seen behind home plate at the Metrodome. The club consigned them to the deep freeze after a couple of games in August, never to be seen again.

It's entirely possible that the only thing worse than a truly ugly baseball uniform is a totally boring baseball uniform. On May 21, 2011, the Boston Red Sox took the field in these throwbacks, which were devoid of any decoration whatsoever.

They were based on their 1918 home set, a look that was both clean and simple—to a fault.

In June 2003, the Boston Red Sox celebrated the 100th anniversary of the inaugural World Series with these floppy-collared numbers, a throwback to a time when some baseball jerseys included lace-up fronts. The originals were far less voluminous than these throwbacks, and the collars were far more modestly proportioned.

The "Turn Back the Clock Day" was delayed two days due to wet weather, but the Red Sox were prepared with these uniforms, which bore a close resemblance to baggy trenchcoats.

The 1998 expansion Tampa Bay Devil Rays emerged into the world in uniforms that perfectly reflected the era. A kaleidoscopic gradient of purple, blue, green, and yellow formed the nucleus of this very '90s-looking set, accompanied by a huge rendering of an ocean-dwelling ray, rendered in that oh so '90s hallmark color, black.

In 2012, the Tampa Bay Rays introduced a uniform that was actually *meant* to be ugly. The Rays, an expansion franchise that played its first game in 1998, rolled out a "fauxback" jersey, a hypothetical look that imagined what the team might have worn had they been around in 1979.

   The look was a not-so-subtle nod to the San Diego Padres' brown and gold disco-era look, repurposed in Rays navy and powder blues. It was all in fun, of course, and it was embraced by many as an imaginative embrace of the golden era of questionable baseball fashion.

On June 16, 2017, Chicago Cubs manager Joe Maddon became the first man to be ejected from a major-league game while dressed as a gas station attendant. This "interesting" look was a throwback tribute to Chicago's Leland Giants, a Negro Leagues powerhouse who played in the earliest years of the twentieth century.

If any club needs or deserves a lager-hued jersey, it's the Milwaukee Brewers. The Brew Crew wore these alternate jerseys for three seasons, from 2013–15, before they were cast aside.

   While the jerseys didn't exactly match the color of Milwaukee's famous liquid gold, they did resemble a grainy Dijon mustard, which would pair up perfectly with a grilled bratwurst and a hoppy IPA.

For one season, 1956, the Cincinnati Redlegs wore this terrifying representation of their mascot on their road uniforms. He looks for all the world like he's going to take a bite out of someone, quite possibly part of some master plan to scare the hell out the rest of the National League.

The team was officially called "Redlegs," as opposed to the familiar "Reds," for several years in the middle of the Cold War, a baseball response to America's antipathy toward the Soviet Union and all things red.

Turning Ahead the Clock

Albert Einstein's theory of general relativity suggests that time travel is indeed possible. Einstein, however, did not live long enough to witness baseball's bold step forward into the 2020s, which—get ready to hop in the DeLorean—took place in the final years of the twentieth century.

On July 18, 1998, the Seattle Mariners turned the clock ahead to the year 2027, a promotional anticipation of the club's long-distant 50th anniversary. The brilliantly inventive Mariners marketing team went all out that night, temporarily redubbing the Kingdome as the "Biodome," and dressing both their team and the visiting Kansas City Royals in campy futuristic uniforms.

What would the uniforms of 2027 look like? Well, for one thing, it would apparently be sleeveless. And shiny. The Mariners' jerseys were black, with an enormous representation of their compass rose logo, tilted counterclockwise at a dynamic angle. Italicized player numbers appeared on the fronts of the jerseys, too, rendered in maroon, a color that was chosen to represent the distant future by none other than Seattle slugger Ken Griffey Jr. himself.

The backs of Seattle's jerseys were also unconventional, with the players' names appearing underneath their numbers, spelt out in wide lowercase letters.

The Royals uniforms were equally memorable. KC wore bright yellow sleeveless jerseys and, like the host Mariners, their pants featured wide stripes on the sides that flared out toward the bottom, until they became one with the players' shoes.

Speaking of shoes, Griffey took a can of metallic silver spray paint to his, as well as those of his teammates. These matched the Mariners' batting helmets, which were matte silver, a fitting matchup for the gold-domed Royals.

The whole exercise was designed to be in good fun, and the theme was embraced with gusto by the home team and fans alike. Several Mariners players, for instance, took Griffey up on his suggestion of wearing their caps backwards and un-tucking their jerseys.

Kevin Martinez, then the Mariners' director of marketing, was the man responsible for the idea. The promotion, he says, was born out of a memorable conversation with Ken Griffey Jr. in 1997.

"We loved the idea of putting a new spin on the 'Turn Back' event," he told me. "Junior was instrumental in picking out the colors of our uniforms. We went all out for our 'Turn Ahead' event—a robot delivered the first pitch ball. James Doohan, the actor who played Scottie in *Star Trek*, was driven out to the mound in a DeLorean through dry ice for the ceremonial first pitch. We created three new inter-planetary teams: the Saturn Rings, the Pluto Mighty Pups, and the Mercury Fire. We added each team's logo to the three American League division standing banners in the outfield. We even included them on the out-of-town scoreboard that night. We borrowed the Astros mascot (the original Orbit) and outfitted him in our 'Turn Ahead' uniform. We used a synthesizer to make the PA announcer sound like a computer. I could go on all day."

What, I asked him, would he change if he had to do it all over again?

"We would revisit the design on the front of the jerseys. We tried to anticipate where design was going and our goal was to make sure the jerseys looked different than anything we had ever seen on the field. In hindsight, it's clear the oversized logo on jerseys hasn't gained any traction. If we could do it again (and we just might one day!) we would design something less gaudy. Oh by the way . . . we accomplished our goal."

The 1998 Seattle Mariners were time-travelling pioneers. One year later, the vast majority of major-league teams joined them when baseball staged a series of "Turn Ahead the Clock" nights, sponsored by the Century 21 real estate firm.

"MLB came to us and wanted to learn more about our event after they saw all the media coverage," Martinez told me. "We explained everything we did. MLB sold the concept to Century 21 for the '99 season. Understandably, most, if not all, of the other clubs didn't love the idea and didn't support it from an event marketing standpoint, so the uniforms became the entire story."

In this instance, the clock was turned ahead to the year 2021. A total of eight clubs opted out, including the reliably austere Yankees with club owner George M. Steinbrenner reportedly saying that the Yankees were already wearing their uniforms of the future.

The promotion certainly got the attention of baseball fans, although much of their reaction was negative—a response to both the corporate association and to the uniforms themselves.

In retrospect, there were plenty of fun, thoughtful details to embrace. The Minnesota Twins, for instance, wore a 60th anniversary sleeve patch. The Oakland Athletics' sleeve patch depicted a menacing-looking Transformers-inspired elephant gripping a bat in its trunk. The St. Louis Cardinals' birds on bat morphed into a metallic, riveted steampunk version of their traditional selves.

The New York Mets shifted the entire franchise to the planet Mercury for the promotion, but their black and silver uniforms did not exactly please the team's players. Rickey Henderson was depicted on the Shea Stadium scoreboard as a pointy-eared three-eyed alien, which drew guffaws from his teammates but a stern rebuke from the future Hall of Famer. Catcher Mike Piazza, reacting to his team's loss to the red-clad Pittsburgh Pirates, noted, "we weren't beamed up to the proper coordinates."

Capped sleeves, huge graphics, and gigantic, tilted logo treatments were (apparently) all to be part of the look of the sport in 2021. Number fonts, in many instances, resembled those seen on digital clocks and VCRs in the waning days of the twentieth century.

Some teams went with vertically oriented player names. Pirates pitcher Pete Schourek told the *Pittsburgh Post-Gazette* that he had a theory about this. "In the future, we're going to quit growing horizontally and we'll grow vertically." Sizing up his futuristic uniform, teammate Brian Giles wondered, "Is this the front?"

The final game of the promotion was supposed to have taken place on September 18 at Fenway Park in Boston, arguably the least futuristic venue imaginable for such a thing. The Red Sox and the visiting Tigers, however, never got to wear their 2021 togs, as the home team's uniform shipment was supposedly delayed by Hurricane Floyd.

In 1950, the Associated Press polled a panel of "experts" who predicted what life would be like in the year 2000. Many of their predictions were prescient, such as the ones that foretold manmade satellites, increased lifespans, and automated, voice-controlled home appliances. Others prognostications, however, were not so accurate. "The woman of the year 2000," they said," will be an outsize Diana . . . she will be more than 6-feet tall, wear a size 11 shoe, have shoulders like a wrestler, and muscles like a truck driver."

Now that the 2020s have officially arrived, what WILL baseball uniforms of the future look like? Here's one man's guess.

Buttons, those vestigial remnants of distant flannelled days of yore, will once again depart the premises. Pictures, rather than words, will increasingly be emphasized, a nod to the fact that society already communicates via abbreviated shorthand. Belts will probably disappear, too, and teams will continue to push the envelope with regard to what uniforms are actually made of.

We will surely continue to see more and more different uniforms, and it seems inevitable that we will see advertising on major-league uniforms sooner rather than later, a move that would follow the National Basketball Association's addition of sponsorship to on-court team uniforms in 2017. Soccer enthusiasts, particularly international fans, will note that ads have been a familiar component of their sport's kits for more than fifty years now. American sports leagues' longstanding reluctance to put advertising front and center seems especially ironic, given our reputation as the preeminent driver of consumer culture worldwide, but the dynamics are rapidly shifting. (The familiar "swoosh" logo of Nike, MLB's new uniform partner, was added to the left chest of all club jerseys in 2020.)

Beyond that, I'd wager that the baseball uniform of the future would still be somewhat recognizable to fans of the 1869 Cincinnati Red Stockings—a shirt, pants, and headwear, as opposed to unitards and space helmets.

That said, the 2027 Seattle Mariners will most likely not be celebrating their actual 50th anniversary in sleeveless jerseys and metallic-hued footwear—but ya never know.

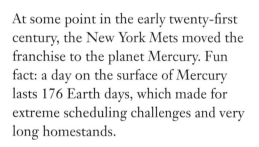

At some point in the early twenty-first century, the New York Mets moved the franchise to the planet Mercury. Fun fact: a day on the surface of Mercury lasts 176 Earth days, which made for extreme scheduling challenges and very long homestands.

Detroit's road uniforms of the future featured a wraparound tiger tail that would have encircled a player number had they ever seen actual game usage (the jerseys were supposedly waylaid in transit due to Hurricane Floyd).

St. Louis' traditional birds-on-bat were transformed into something from a dystopian science fiction movie with an avian theme.

The Arizona Diamondbacks TATC look was an inspired one, even if player names and numbers were a little difficult to read.

The Brewers' "Turn Ahead the Clock" jerseys contained a bizarre mix of past, present, and future. The club paired their original "barrelman" mascot with their then-current team lettering, placed atop the imagined jersey template of 2021, thus covering all time-travel bases in one neat package.

"I JUST WISH THAT
THE GUYS WHO ORDERED THESE
WOULD HAVE TO WEAR THEM."
--DAVE McNALLY

8:03 **AT BAT** 8 **OUTS** 1 **BALLS** 2 **STRIKES** 1

HOT PANTS DAY JULY 24

Conclusion

Baseball fans' love (and hate) for their team's uniforms could well be the topic of an entirely different book. As I have previously noted, people have been opining about the on-field look of the game since its earliest days. What's different now, however, is the fact that the fans—at least some of them—actually dress like the players.

Sepia-toned photos of baseball games from the distant past recall a far more formal age. Images of crowds attending the first World Series in 1903 reveal a sea of elegantly dressed men, many wearing bowler hats. Jump forward six or seven decades and we see a more diverse group of fans, dressed far more causally. While some may have swapped fancy antique headwear for baseball caps, jerseys are nowhere to be seen.

That all changed in the late 1980s when Major League Baseball and Rawlings teamed up to bring authentic togs to the masses, and things haven't been the same since. The idea of fans—especially adult fans—wearing replica jerseys would have been a laughable concept back in the more buttoned-up days of yore. Attend any game, anywhere, today and you will witness a significant number of spectators dressed up in a dizzying array of jerseys.

The wearing of an authentic jersey reinforces the already powerful tribal connection that fans feel for their teams. Customized jerseys take this relationship to the next level, symbolically propelling a fan onto the 40-man roster.

Another phenomenon began to unfold at the precise moment that the market for replica jerseys was exploding in the early 1990s. Jerseys from baseball's ancient past began to resurface in the form of replicas, manufactured and sold by Philadelphia-based Mitchell & Ness as part of Major League Baseball's "Cooperstown Collection."

I purchased Mitchell & Ness's 1991 catalog and I still own it. It's a thing of beauty, 10 inches square and glossy, and it's filled with dozens of photographs that evoke baseball's mythic history. The images crammed full of felt and flannel, embroidered patches, old newspapers and scorecards, worn leather mitts and weathered bats. The jackets and jerseys are gorgeous, and the most recent replica is from 1969.

Their next catalog, which was released in 1995, is still dominated by a range of offerings from the olden days, but they are accompanied by a smattering of doubleknits, including a green Oakland A's jersey and a 1985 White Sox "beach blanket." All of that leads us to the 1998 version, which features the Astros' rainbows, an orange Giants jersey, a bright yellow Padres jersey, and a bunch of other reproductions of jerseys from baseball's most colorful era.

The nostalgia market was initially geared toward aging baby boomers, folks who identified with the flannelled era of Willie, Mickey, and The Duke. By the turn of the new millennium the focus had shifted to what retailers called "the urban market," fueled by the very visible and culturally influential world of rap and hip hop.

Jay-Z wore an early '80s San Diego Padres jersey. Outkast famously embraced the Astros' rainbow look. Rappers from coast-to-coast sported powder blue throwbacks from the '70s and '80s. Hip-hop gave exposure and a newfound sense of appreciation to some of the ugliest baseball uniforms ever worn and the market responded with vigor. Mitchell & Ness's sales boomed, rising from $1.5 million in 1998 to $23 million only four years later.

Attend a Major League game in Milwaukee these days and you'll encounter a surprisingly large number of fans sporting the Brewers' old ball-in-glove logo, which was tweaked and brought back full-time in 2020. Walk through the stands at a game in Philadelphia and you'll be joined by a ton of folks wearing powder blue Phillies apparel with the club's maroon "swirly P," a '70s and '80s mainstay that was revived as an alternate uniform in 2019. There's a curious dynamic at play here. I saw the Pirates' bumblebee uniforms in person back in the '70s. I am old enough to have witnessed the White Sox at the peak of their floppy-collared glory. Some of baseball's most "questionable" uniforms of the past are now being embraced with vigor by a whole new generation—and this is a good thing.

It's easy to recall and appreciate the classics. Baseball's past is often viewed through a gauzy veil of nostalgia, and there's no disputing the beauty of the Yankees' pinstripes, the Red Sox' handsome scarlet-trimmed uniforms, or the Tigers' always-fashionable Old English "D."

With that said, let's lift a toast to the outliers, the oddballs, the weirdoes, and the misfits. And let's give praise to those of us who, in a world full of relentless conformity, have the ability to see things differently.

My daughters, Hannah and Kate, merit mention here, too. I schlepped them to many a game in their younger years. In fact, Hannah and I saw the final contest ever played by the Montreal Expos, at Shea Stadium in New York in 2004. I explained their logo as best I could, fatherly duties somewhat accomplished.

Finally, acknowledgment must be given to Susanne Reece, who, at the outset of the project, gave me some simple but invaluable advice. "Write, just write. And keep writing."

I did.

Todd Radom is a graphic designer, professional sports branding expert, and writer. He has created official logos and graphic identities for many professional sports teams and events, including for Major League Baseball, and has provided commentary on sports branding for publications such as the *New York Times*.